Sumatra

Paul Dixon

Credits

Footprint credits
Editor: Felicity Laughton
Production and layout: Emma Bryers
Maps: Kevin Feeney

Managing Director: Andy Riddle
Commercial Director: Patrick Dawson
Publisher: Alan Murphy
Publishing Managers: Felicity Laughton,
Jo Williams, Nicola Gibbs
Marketing and Partnerships Director:
Liz Harper
Marketing Executive: Liz Eyles
Trade Product Manager: Diane McEntee
Account Managers: Paul Bew, Tania Ross
Advertising: Renu Sibal, Elizabeth Taylor
Trade Product Co-ordinator: Kirsty Holmes

Photography credits
Front cover: Dreamstime
Back cover: Shutterstock

Printed in the United States of America

Publishing information
Footprint *Focus Sumatra*
1st edition
© Footprint Handbooks Ltd
September 2012

ISBN: 978 1 908206 85 5
CIP DATA: A catalogue record for this book
is available from the British Library

® Footprint Handbooks and the Footprint
mark are a registered trademark of
Footprint Handbooks Ltd

Published by Footprint
6 Riverside Court
Lower Bristol Road
Bath BA2 3DZ, UK
T +44 (0)1225 469141
F +44 (0)1225 469461
footprinttravelguides.com

Distributed in the USA by Globe Pequot
Press, Guilford, Connecticut

Every effort has been made to ensure that
the facts in this guidebook are accurate.
However, travellers should still obtain advice
from consulates, airlines, etc, about travel
and visa requirements before travelling.
The authors and publishers cannot accept
responsibility for any loss, injury or
inconvenience however caused.

The content of Footprint *Focus Sumatra*
has been taken directly from Footprint's
Southeast Asia Handbook which was
researched and written by Andrew Spooner
and Paul Dixon.

Although Sumatra does not have Java's historical and archaeo-logical sights, it does offer magnificent natural landscapes. Perhaps most spectacular of all is the upland crater lake of Danau Toba. The forests, mountains, rivers and coasts all provide great trekking and rafting opportunities, some of the finest national parks in the country and pristine beaches.

There are also over a dozen ethnic groups on the island, who speak some 20 different dialects, including the peripatetic Minangkabau of West Sumatra, the Christian Bataks of North Sumatra, the Ferrant Muslims of Aceh and the tribal peoples of Nias and Mentawi.

As the world's fourth-largest island (nearly 475,000 sq km), Sumatra also acts as a 'safety valve' for Java's 'excess' population. About 60% of Indonesia's transmigrants – four million people – have been resettled on Sumatra, mostly in the south. Population densities here are less than one-tenth of those on neighbouring Java, although some areas – such as Lampung province – are beginning to suffer the effects of overcrowding.

Sumatra is also crucial to the Indonesian economy. It was in North Sumatra that Indonesia's first commercial oil well was sunk in 1871, and over 60% of the country's total petroleum and gas production comes from the island and the seas that surround it.

Planning your trip

Where to go in Sumatra

Travelling in Sumatra can be a time-consuming business. Some key destinations – notably Danau Toba – have no airport. Furthermore, distances can be great and, with average road speeds of around 50 kph, even on the Trans-Sumatran 'highway', it can take a while to get from A to B. This means that anyone intending to sample Sumatra in anything more than the most cursory of ways will need to allocate at least 10 days. The classic 'route' is to travel between Medan and Padang (which both have airports with daily flights), via Berastagi, Danau Toba and Bukittinggi. This really requires a minimum of 10 days and preferably two weeks. However, there are opportunities for shorter stays, and people living in the region regularly come to Sumatra for a week or less for breaks in the cool Batak and Minang highlands. It is quite feasible to fly into Medan and make for Danau Toba for five days or to Padang and take the bus up to Bukittinggi for a similar length of time. Long-haul visitors, with jet lag to deal with and perhaps a new climate too, would probably find such a short visit exhausting and ultimately less than satisfying.

Best time to visit Sumatra

Sumatra's climate varies considerably across the island. North of the equator the rainy season extends from October to April, and south of the equator from October to January. Road travel during the dry season is quicker and easier, but overland travel in the wet season is fine on the (largely) all-weather Trans-Sumatran Highway. Most tourists visit between June and October, so travelling out of those months is relatively quiet and hotel rates can often be bargained down.

Getting to Sumatra

Air
Most visitors arrive at Medan, in the north, near the west coast of Sumatra, which offers international connections with Kuala Lumpur (KLIA and Subang), Penang, Hong Kong, Bangkok and Singapore. There are also flights from Singapore to Padang. There are domestic connections with Jakarta from all Sumatran provincial capitals.

Boat
The handy Belawan (Medan's port) to Penang international ferry service and the Belawan to Lumut (in Perak, Malaysia) have both been suspended. Check with agents around town for the latest, although it is unlikely these lines will be restored given the number of cheap airlines flying over the Straits. An alternative route into or out of Indonesia is to catch a regular high-speed ferry from Singapore's World Trade Centre or Tanah Merah pier to Batam or Bintan islands in the Riau archipelago (40 minutes). From there it is possible to catch a boat – fast or very slow – to Pekanbaru, up the Siak River on the Sumatran 'mainland', from where it is a five-hour bus ride to Bukitinggi. There are also ferry connections between Melaka and Dumai, although this is not a very popular entry/exit point. The most important domestic entry/exit point is Bakauheni on Sumatra's south

Don't miss...

tip; hourly ferries link Bakauheni with Merak (West Java). The **PELNI** ship *Kelud* calls in on Belawan on loops to Jakarta's Tanjung Priok via Balai Karimun and Batam respectively.

Transport in Sumatra

Air

This is the most convenient and comfortable way to travel around Sumatra. **Garuda** and **Merpati** service all the main provincial cities. The other main domestic airlines on Sumatra are **Lion Air** and **Kartika**. Smallest of all are **SMAC** and **Susi Air**, which tend to service more out-of-the-way places.

Bus

Buses are the main mode of long-distance travel. Steady improvements to the 2500-km Trans-Sumatran 'Highway' (a misnomer – some sections are more like a village road, 1½ lanes wide), which runs down the entire island from Banda Aceh in the north to Bakauheni in the south, are making road travel much faster and more comfortable. It used to take 20 hours to travel from Parapat to Bukittinggi, now it takes 10-14 hours depending on the vehicle. Roads off the Trans-Sumatran Highway are still generally poor, and in the rainy season delays of two days are not unknown while floodwaters subside. Travelling through the Bukit Barisan, or along the west coast, is still quite slow, with average speeds of 40-50 kph, as the road follows every turn of the mountain. There are air-conditioned, VIP or express buses plying all the major routes. The most highly regarded private bus companies are **ALS** and **ANS**.

Tourist buses also now ply the popular routes. In particular, the route from Padang, through Berastagi, Danau Toba and Sibolga, to Bukittinggi. These *bis parawisata* (tourist buses) are often eight-seat minibuses that leave at a set hour (roughly) and tend to arrive more quickly than the *bis biasa* (ordinary bus) alternatives. Tourist services are safer; they often pick up and drop off at hotels in towns; and they may also include stops at designated tourist sights en route (the dreaded *objek wisata*). The main disadvantage (other than cost) is that they reduce contact between locals and tourists.

Train

There is a limited rail network in Sumatra. In the north, there is a line running from Medan to Rantau Parapat, and from Medan to Tanjung Balai

Where to stay in Sumatra

Tourist and business centres usually have a good range of accommodation for all budgets. However, visitors venturing off the beaten track may find hotels restricted to dingy and overpriced establishments catering for local businessmen and officials. The best-run and most competitively priced budget accommodation is found in popular tourist spots. It is almost always worth bargaining. This is particularly true for hotels in tourist destinations that attract a fair amount of local weekend business: the weekday room rate may be 50% less than the weekend rate. All hotels are required to display their room rates (for every category of room) on a *daftar harga*, or price list. This is invariably either in public view in the reception area or will be produced when you ask about room rates. Indonesians prefer to be on the ground floor, so rooms on higher floors are usually cheaper. In cheaper accommodation, the bed may consist only of a bottom sheet and pillow with no top sheet.

Terminology can be confusing: a *losmen* is a lower price range hotel (in parts of Sumatra *losmen* are known as *penginapan*); a *wisma* is a guesthouse, but these can range in price from cheap to moderately expensive; finally, a *hotel* is a hotel, but can range from the cheap and squalid up to a Hilton.

With the economy faring well in Indonesia in recent years, and a more affluent middle class emerging, mid-range and top-end hotels are being built at an extraordinary rate, many offering excellent promotion rates and possessing all the mod cons an international traveller requires. The backpacker market has seen less money being poured into it than, for example, in Malaysia and Thailand, and these places can often seem to be a bit bleak and tawdry compared to cheaper digs elsewhere in Southeast Asia.

Bathing and toilets

Baths and showers are not a feature of many cheaper *losmen*. Instead a *mandi* (a water tank and ladle) is used to wash. The tub is not climbed into; water is ladled from the tub and splashed over the head. The traditional Asian toilet is of the squat variety. (Toilets are called *kamar kecil* – the universal 'small room' – or *way say*, as in the initials 'WC'.) Toilet paper is not traditionally used; the faithful left hand and water suffice. In cheaper accommodation you are expected to bring your own towels, soap and toilet paper.

Food and drink in Sumatra

Food

The main staple across the archipelago is rice. Today, alternatives such as corn, sweet potatoes and sago, which are grown primarily in the dry islands of the East, are regarded as 'poor man's food', and rice is the preferred staple.

Indonesians will eat rice – or *nasi* (milled, cooked rice) – at least three times a day. Breakfast is often left-over rice, stir-fried and served up as *nasi goreng*. Mid-morning snacks are often sticky rice cakes or *pisang goreng* (fried bananas). Rice is the staple for lunch, served up with two or three meat and vegetable dishes and followed by fresh fruit. The main meal is supper, which is served quite early and again consists of rice, this time accompanied by as many as five or six other dishes. *Sate/satay* (grilled skewers of meat), *soto* (a nourishing soup) or *bakmi* (noodles, a dish of Chinese origin) may be served first.

In many towns *sate*, *soto* or *bakmi* vendors roam the streets with carts containing charcoal braziers, ringing a bell or hitting a block (the noise will signify what he or she

Price codes

Where to stay

$$$$	over US$100	$$$	US$46-100
$$	US$21-45	$	US$20 and under

Price codes refer to the cost of a standard double/twin room in high season.

Restaurants

$$$ over US$12		$$ US$6-12	$ under US$6

Price codes refer to the cost of a two-course meal, not including drinks.

is selling) in the early evenings. These carts are known as *kaki lima* (five legs). *Pedagang* (vendor) *kaki lima* also refers to hawkers who peddle their wares from stalls and from baskets hung from shoulder poles.

Larger foodstalls tend to set up in the same place every evening in a central position in town. These *warungs*, as they are known, may be temporary structures or more permanent buildings, with simple tables and benches. In the larger cities, there may be an area of *warungs*, all under one roof. Often a particular street will become known as the best place to find particular dishes like *martabak* (savoury meat pancakes) or *gado gado* (vegetable salad served with peanut sauce). More formalized restaurants are known simply as *rumah makan* (literally 'eating houses'), often shortened to just 'RM'. A good place to look for cheap stall food is in and around the market or *pasar*; night markets or *pasar malam* are usually better for eating than day markets.

Feast days, such as Lebaran marking the end of Ramadan, are a cause for great celebration and traditional dishes are served. *Lontong* or *ketupat* are made at this time (they are both versions of boiled rice – simmered in a small container or bag, so that as it cooks, the rice is compressed to make a solid block). This may be accompanied by *rendang* (curried beef) in Sumatra. *Nasi kuning* (yellow rice) is traditionally served at a *selamatan* (a Javanese celebration marking a birth, the collection of the rice harvest or the completion of a new house).

In addition to rice, there are a number of other common ingredients used across the country. Coconut milk, ginger, chilli peppers and peanuts are used nationwide, while dried salted fish and soybeans are important sources of protein. In coastal areas, fish and seafood tend to be more important than meat. As Indonesia is more than 80% Muslim, pork is not widely eaten (except in Chinese restaurants) but in some regions, such as the area around Lake Toba in Sumatra, it is much more in evidence.

Regional cuisines

Although Indonesia is becoming more homogeneous as Javanese culture spreads to the Outer Islands, there are still distinctive regional cuisines. The food of Java embraces a number of regional forms, of which the most distinctive is **Sundanese**. *Lalap*, a Sundanese dish, consists of raw vegetables and is said to be the only Indonesian dish where vegetables are eaten uncooked. Characteristic ingredients of Javanese dishes are soybeans, beef, chicken and vegetables; characteristic flavours are an interplay of sweetness and spiciness. Probably the most famous regional cuisine, however, is **Padang** or **Minang** food, which has its origins in West Sumatra province. Padang food has 'colonized' the rest of the country and there are Padang restaurants in every town, no matter how small. Dishes tend to be hot and spicy, using quantities of chilli and turmeric, and include *rendang* (dry beef curry), *kalo ayam* (creamy chicken curry) and *dendeng balado* (fried seasoned sun-dried meat with a spicy coating). There are large numbers of Chinese people scattered across the archipelago and, like other countries of the region, **Chinese** restaurants are widespread.

Drink

Water must be boiled for at least five minutes before it is safe to drink. Hotels and most restaurants should boil the water they offer customers. Ask for *air minum* (drinking water). Many restaurants provide a big jug of boiled water on each table. In cheaper establishments it is probably best to play safe and ask for bottled water, although consider the environmental impact of this.

'**Mineral water**' – of which the most famous is *Aqua* ('aqua' has become the generic word for mineral water) – is available in all but the smallest and most remote towns. Check the seal is intact before accepting a bottle. Bottled water is cheap, and considerably cheaper at supermarkets than at the many kiosks lining the streets.

Western **bottled and canned drinks** are widely available in Indonesia and are comparatively cheap. Alternatively, most restaurants will serve *air jeruk* (citrus **fruit juices**) with or without ice (*es*). The **coconut milk** is a good thirst quencher and a good source of potassium and glucose. Fresh fruit juices vary greatly in quality; some are little more than water, sugar and ice. Ice in many places is fine, but in cheaper restaurants and away from tourist areas many people recommend taking drinks without ice. Javanese, Sumatran, Sulawesi or Timorese *kopi* (coffee), fresh and strong, is an excellent morning pick-you-up. It is usually served *kopi manis* (sweet) and black; if you want to have it without sugar, ask for it *tidak pakai gula*. The same goes for other drinks habitually served with mountains of sugar (like fruit juices). *Susu* (milk) is available in tourist areas and large towns, but it may be sweetened condensed milk. *Teh* (tea), usually weak, is obtainable almost everywhere. *Teh jahe* (hot ginger tea) is a refreshing alternative.

Although Indonesia is a predominantly Muslim country, alcohol is widely available. The two most popular **beers** – light lagers – are the locally brewed *Anker* and *Bintang* brands. Wine is becoming more popular. A reasonable bottle can be bought for around US$15. Imported **spirits** are comparatively expensive, however, a number of local brews including *brem* (rice wine), *arak* (rice whisky) and *tuak* (palm wine) are available.

Local customs and laws

As a rule, Indonesians are courteous and understanding. Visitors should be the same. Foreigners are often given the benefit of the doubt when norms are transgressed. However, it is best to have a grasp of at least the basics of accepted behaviour. There are also some areas – such as Aceh in North Sumatra – that are more fervently Muslim than other parts of the country. With such a diverse array of cultures and religions, accepted conduct varies. Generally, the more popular an area is (as a tourist destination) the more understanding local people are likely to be of tourist habits. But this is not to imply that anything goes. It is also true that familiarity can breed contempt, so even in places like Bali it is important to be sensitive to the essentials of local culture.

Calmness Like other countries of Southeast Asia, a calm attitude is highly admired, especially if things are going wrong. Keep calm and cool when bargaining, or waiting for a delayed bus or appointment. •

Dress Indonesia is largely a Muslim country. Dress modestly and avoid shorts, short skirts and sleeveless dresses or shirts (except at the beach). Public nudity and topless bathing are not acceptable. Light clothing is suitable all year round, except at night in the mountains. Proper decorum should be observed when visiting places of worship; shorts are not permitted in mosques, shoulders and arms should be covered, and women must cover their heads. Formal dress for men normally consists of a batik shirt and trousers; suits are rarely worn. Local women usually wear a *kebaya*.

Face People should not be forced to lose face in public; especially in front of colleagues. Putting someone in a position of *malu* or social shame should be avoided.

Gifts If you are invited to somebody's home, it is customary to take a gift. This is not opened until after the visitor has left. Most small general stores have a range of pre-wrapped and boxed gifts, appropriate for a variety of occasions including weddings. These are usually items of china or glasses.

Heads, hands and feet The head is considered sacred and should never be touched (especially those of children). Handshaking is common among both men and women, but the use of the left hand to give or receive is taboo. When eating with fingers, use the right hand only. Pointing with your finger is impolite; use your thumb to point. Beckon buses (or any person) with a flapping motion of your right hand down by your side. When sitting with others, do not cross your legs; it is considered disrespectful. Do not point with your feet and keep them off tables. Remove shoes when entering houses.

Open affection Public displays of affection between men and women are considered objectionable. However, Indonesians of the same sex tend to be affectionate – holding hands, for example.

Punctuality *Jam karet* or 'rubber time' is a peculiarly Indonesian phenomenon. Patience and a cool head are very important; appointments are rarely at the time arranged.

Religion Indonesia is the largest Muslim country in the world. Orthodox Islam is strongest in northern Sumatra, but is also present in parts of Sulawesi, Kalimantan and West Java. Since the Bali bombings and suicide attacks in Jakarta, Islam in Indonesia, and the *pesentren* (Islamic boarding schools – the most famous being Al-Mukmin Ngruki in Java with graduates including the Bali bombers) have been put under the microscope with the government keen to disassociate itself with any links to fundamentalist groups. However, the government has so far proved itself unable to stop radical groups agitating, despite placing huge emphasis on intelligence and anti-terror schemes.

Mosques are sacred houses of prayer; non-Muslims can enter a mosque, so long as they observe the appropriate customs: remove shoes before entering, dress appropriately, do not disturb the peace, and do not walk too close to or in front of somebody who is praying. During the fasting month of Ramadan, do not eat, drink or smoke in the presence of Muslims during daylight hours.

Bali has remained a **Hindu** island, and remnants of Hinduism are also evident in parts of Central and East Java. To enter a temple or *pura* on Bali, it is often necessary to wear a sash around the waist (at some temples a sarong is also required); these are available for hire at the more popular temples, or can be bought for about 10,000Rp (20,000Rp for a sarong). Modest and tidy dress is also required when visiting Hindu temples; women should not enter wearing short dresses or with bare shoulders. Do not use flash during ceremonies. Women menstruating are requested not to enter temples.

Pockets of **Christianity** can be found throughout the archipelago, notably in East Nusa Tenggara, around Danau Toba and Sulawesi. Evangelical Christianity is enjoying large numbers of converts among the ethnic Chinese.

Festivals in Sumatra → *Muslim festivals are based on the lunar calendar.*

January
Tahun Baru, New Year's Day (1st: public holiday). **New Year's Eve** is celebrated with street carnivals, shows, fireworks and all-night festivities. In Christian areas, festivities are more exuberant, with people visiting each other on New Year's Day and attending church services.

January/February
Imlek, Chinese New Year (movable, 10 Feb 2013). An official holiday; many Chinese shops and businesses close for at least 2 days. Within the Chinese community, younger people visit their relatives, children are given *hong bao* (lucky money), new clothes are bought and any unfinished business is cleared up.

March/April
Garebeg Maulad, or Maulud Nabi Muhammed, birthday of the Prophet

Mohammad (movable, 24 Jan 2013: public holiday), to commemorate Prophet Muhammad's birthday in AD 571. Processions and Koran recitals in most big towns. Celebrations begin a week before the actual day and last a month, with *selamatans* in homes, mosques and schools. **Wafat Isa Al-Masih**, Good Friday (movable, 29 March 2013: public holiday). **Kartini Day** (21 Apr). A ceremony held by women to mark the birthday of Raden Ajeng Kartini, born in 1879 and proclaimed as a pioneer of women's emancipation. Women are supposed to be pampered by their husbands and children, although it is women's organizations like the Dharma Wanita who get most excited. Women wear national dress.

May
Waisak Day (movable, 25 May 2013: public holiday). Marks the birth and death of the

historic Buddha; at Candi Mendut outside Yogyakarta, a procession of monks carrying flowers, candles, holy fire and images of the Buddha walk to Borobudur.
Kenaikan Isa Al-Masih or Ascension Day (movable, 9 May 2013: public holiday).

June/July
Al Miraj or Isra Miraj Nabi Muhammed (movable, 5 June 2013). The ascension of the Prophet Mohammad when he is led through the 7 heavens by the archangel. He speaks with God and returns to earth the same night, with instructions that include the 5 daily prayers.

July/August
Awal Ramadan (movable, 9 July 2013). The 1st day of Ramadan, a month of fasting for all Muslims. Muslims abstain from all food, drink and smoking from sunrise to sundown – if they are very strict, Muslims do not even swallow their own saliva during daylight hours. It is strictly adhered to in more conservative areas like Aceh and West Sumatra, and many restaurants remain closed during daylight hours – making life tiresome for non-Muslims. Every evening for 30 days before breaking of fast, stalls selling traditional Malay cakes and delicacies are set up. The only people exempt from fasting are the elderly, those who are travelling and women who are pregnant or menstruating.
Independence Day (17 Aug: public holiday). The most important national holiday, celebrated with processions and dancing. Although it's officially on 17 Aug, festivities continue for a month, towns are decorated with bunting and parades cause delays to bus travel, there seems to be no way of knowing when each town will hold its parades.

September
Idul Fitri (Aidil Fitri) or **Lebaran** (movable, 9 Aug 2013: public holiday) is a 2-day celebration that marks the end of Ramadan, and is a period of prayer and celebration. In order for Hari Raya to be declared, the new moon of Syawal has to be sighted; if it is not, fasting continues for another day. It is the most important time of the year for Muslim families. Mass prayers are held in mosques and squares. Public transport is booked up weeks in advance and hotels are often full.

October
Hari Pancasila (1 Oct). This commemorates the Five Basic Principles of Pancasila.
Armed Forces Day (5 Oct). The anniversary of the founding of the Indonesian Armed Forces; military parades and demonstrations.

November/December
Idhul Adha (movable, 15 Oct 2013: public holiday). Celebrated by Muslims to mark the 10th day of Zulhijgah, the 12th month of the Islamic calendar when pilgrims celebrate their return from the Haj to Mecca. In the morning, prayers are offered; later, families hold 'open house'. This is the 'festival of the sacrifice'. Burial graves are cleaned, and an animal is sacrificed to be distributed to the poor to commemorate the willingness of Abraham to sacrifice his son. Indonesian men who have made the pilgrimage to Mecca wear a white skull-hat.
Muharram (movable, 14 Nov 2012, 4 Nov 2013: public holiday), Muslim New Year. Marks the 1st day of the Muslim calendar and celebrates the Prophet Muhammad's journey from Mecca to Medina on the lunar equivalent of AD 16 Jul 622.
Christmas Day (25 Dec: public holiday). Celebrated by Christians – the Bataks of Sumatra, the Toraja and Minahasans of Sulawesi and in some of the islands of Nusa Tenggara, and Irian Jaya.

Shopping in Sumatra

Indonesia offers a wealth of distinctive handicrafts and other products. Best buys include textiles (batik and *ikat*), silverwork, woodcarving, *krisses* (indigenous daggers), puppets, paintings and ceramics. Bali has the greatest choice of handicrafts. It is not necessarily the case that you will find the best buys in the area where a particular product is made; the larger cities sell a wide range of handicrafts and antiques from across the archipelago at competitive prices.

Tips on buying

Early morning sales may well be cheaper, as salespeople often believe the first sale augurs well for the rest of the day. Except in the larger fixed-price stores, bargaining (with good humour) is expected; start at 60% lower than the asking price. Do not expect to achieve instant results; if you walk away from the shop, you will almost certainly be followed, with a lower offer. If the salesperson agrees to your price, you should feel obliged to purchase – it is considered very ill mannered to agree on a price and then not buy the article.

Essentials A-Z

Accident and emergency
Ambulance T118, Fire T113, Police T110.

Electricity
220-240 volts, 50 cycle. 2 types of plug:
2 round pins or 2 parallel flat pins with
ground pin (UK style).

Embassies and consulates
Visit www.embassygoabroad.com
for a full list of embassies.

Language
The national language is Bahasa Indonesia,
which is written in Roman script. There are
250 regional languages and dialects, of
which Sundanese (the language of West
Java and Jakarta) is the most widespread.
In Padang and elsewhere in West Sumatra,
the population speak Minang, which is
also similar to Bahasa. About 70% of the
population can speak Bahasa. English is
the most common foreign language, with
some Dutch and Portuguese speakers.

Bahasa Indonesia is relatively easy to
learn, a small number of useful words and
phrases are listed in the box, on page 16.

Money → *US$1 = 9475Rp (Aug 2012).*
For latest rates, visit www.xe.com.
The unit of currency in Indonesia is the
rupiah (Rp). When taking US$ in cash, make
sure the bills are new and crisp, as banks
in Indonesia can be fussy about which bills
they accept (Sumatra is particularly bad).
Larger denomination US$ bills also tend to
command a premium exchange rate. In more
out of the way places it is worth making sure
that you have a stock of smaller notes and
coins – it can be hard to break larger bills.

Two of the better banks are **Bank Negara
Indonesia (BNI)** and **Bank Central Asia (BCA)**.
BNI is reliable and efficient and most of their

branches will change US$ TCs. Banks in larger
towns and tourist centres have ATMs. Cash
or traveller's cheques (TCs) can be changed
in most tourist centres at a competitive rate.
Credit cards are widely accepted.

Tipping is commonplace in Indonesia,
and small bills are often handed over at
the end of every transaction to smooth it
over and ensure good service, Indeed, it
can often seem that the whole country is
founded on tipping, an informal way of
channelling money through society so that
lower earners can supplement their meagre
earnings and are motivated into action.
A 10% service charge is added to bills at
more expensive hotels. Porters expect to
be tipped about 2000Rp a bag. In more
expensive restaurants, where no service is
charged, a tip of 5-10% may be appropriate.
Taxi drivers (in larger towns) appreciate a
small tip (1000Rp). *Parkirs* always expect
payment for 'watching' your vehicle; 1000Rp.

Cost of travelling
Indonesia is no longer the bargain country
it was 10 years ago. Whilst it is still cheap
by Western standards tourists can now
expect to dig deeper for their meals
and accommodation. Visitors staying in
1st-class hotels and eating in top-notch
restaurants will probably spend between
US100 and US$150 a day. Tourists on a
mid-range budget, staying in cheaper
a/c accommodation and eating in local
restaurants, will probably spend between
US$50-80 a day. A backpacker, staying in
fan-cooled guesthouses and eating cheaply,
could scrape by on US$20-25 a day, though
this leaves little room for wild partying.
Indonesia has seen prices spiral in recent
years, particularly for food and this is reflected
in the increased costs that travellers now have
to bear when visiting the country.

Useful words and phrases

Pronunciation is not difficult as there is a close relationship between the way the letter is written and the sound. Stress is usually on the second syllable.

You will be asked constantly 'Where are you going?' (Mau ke mana?) as it is a common form of Indonesian address. Try saying 'cuci mata' ('washing my eye'), which means relaxing, or 'makan angin' ('eating the air').

Yes/no	*Ya/tidak*
Thank you	*Terima kasi h*
Excuse me, sorry!	*Ma'af*
Welcome	*Selamat datang*
Good morning	*Selamat pagi*
Good afternoon	*Selamat sore*
Good evening	*Selamat malam*
Where's the ...?	*... dimana?*
How much is ...?	*... berapa harganya?*
I (don't) understand	*Saya (tidak) mengerti*

Safety

Despite the recent media coverage of terrorist plots and attacks, riots and other disturbances in Indonesia, it remains a safe country and violence against foreigners is rare. Petty theft is a minor problem.

Avoid carrying large amounts of cash; TCs can be changed in most major towns.

Beware of the confidence tricksters who are widespread in tourist areas. Sudden reports of unbeatable bargains or closing down sales are usual ploys.

Civil unrest Embassies ask visitors to exercise caution when travelling in Aceh, a region recovering from a long internal conflict.

Flying After a series of accidents the EU banned many Indonesian airlines from entering its air space over continuing concerns of poor maintenance and safety. The Indonesian government and airline companies have taken this very seriously and the last few years have seen brand new Boeings and Airbuses being rolled out by **Lion Air** and **Garuda**. The airlines considered acceptable by the EU are **Batavia**, **Garuda** and **Indonesia AirAsia**. Many European embassies advise against domestic air travel. For the latest information, see www.fco.gov.uk/en and www.travel.state.gov/travel/warnings.html.

Tax

Expect to pay 11% tax in the more expensive restaurants. Some cheaper restaurants serving foreigners may add 10% to the bill.

Airport tax 75,000Rp-150,000Rp on international flights, and anywhere between 10,000Rp and 30,000Rp on domestic flights, depending on the airport.

Telephone → *Country code +62.*

Operator T101. International enquiries T102. Local enquiries T108. Long-distance enquiries T106. Every town has its communication centres (**Wartel**), where you can make local and international calls and faxes.

Mobile phones Known as hand-phones or HP in Indonesia, use has sky rocketed and costs are unbelievably low. It usually costs around 15,000Rp to by a Sim card with a number. Top-up cards are sold at various denominations. If you buy a 10,000Rp or 20,000Rp card, the vendor will charge a few more thousand, in order to gain some profit. If you buy a 100,000Rp card, you will pay a few thousand less than 100,000Rp. This is standard practice throughout the country. Reliable operators include **Telkomsel**, **IM3** and **Pro XL**. If you want to buy a dirt cheap phone in country, look for the Esia brand which offers bargain basement phone and credit packages.

Visas and immigration

Visitors from several nations, including Malaysia, The Philippines and Singapore are allowed a visa-free stay of 30 days in Indonesia. Visitors from nations including the following are able to get a US$25 30-day **Visa On Arrival (VOA)**: Australia, Canada, France, Germany, Holland, Ireland, Italy, New Zealand, Portugal, Spain, United Kingdom and the USA. Check with your embassy. Pay at a booth at the port of entry. These visas are extendable at immigration offices in the country for an extra 30 days. Visitors wishing to obtain a VOA must enter and leave Indonesia though certain ports of entry, including the following:

Sea ports Batam, Tanjung Uban, Belawan (Medan), Dumai, Jayapura, Tanjung Balaikarimun, Bintang Pura (Tanjung Pinang), and Kupang.

Airports Medan, Pekanbaru, Padang, Jakarta, Surabaya, Bali, Manado, Adisucipto in Yogyakarta, Adisumarmo in Solo, and Selaparang in Mataram, Lombok.

60-day visitor visas (B211) are available at Indonesian embassies and consulates around the world (a ticket out of the country, 2 photos and a completed visa form is necessary). Costs vary. They can be extended giving a total stay of 6 months (must be extended at an immigration office in Indonesia each month after the initial 60-day visa has expired; take it to the office 4 days before expiry). To extend the visa in Indonesia, a fee of US$25 is levied and a sponsor letter from a local person is needed. To obtain a 60-day visitor visa in Singapore, a one-way ticket from Batam to Singapore is adequate: purchase from the ferry centre at HarbourFront in Singapore.

It is crucial to check this information before travelling as the visa situation in Indonesia is extremely volatile. Travellers who overstay their visa will be fined US$20 a day. Long-term overstayers can expect a fine and jail sentence. See www.indonesian embassy.org.uk for more information.

All visitors to Indonesia must possess a passport valid for at least 6 months from their date of arrival in Indonesia, and they should have proof of onward travel. It is not uncommon for immigration officers to ask to see a ticket out of the country. (A Batam–Singapore ferry ticket or cheap Medan–Penang air ticket will suffice).

Contents

Sumatra

Medan

Medan is big, hot, noisy, congested and dirty, with only a few havens of greenery – for example, Merdeka Square – and no obvious 'sights' to enthrall the visitor. However, while the architecture is not notable by international standards it is significant in the Indonesian context, and Medan does provide a vivid and vivacious introduction to Asia for those who are new to the region. In addition, and perhaps because foreign tourists are less in evidence, the local people are generally warm and welcoming. For those coming from other parts of Indonesia, Medan shows the country in quite a different light, sharing plenty in common with Peninsular Malaysia. This is evident in the crumbling Chinese shophouses, with their low walkways and the smell of incense wafting out into the street. Visitors will also note the presence of a permanent Indian population, not seen anywhere else in the archipelago, driving becaks (rickshaws), cooking fine curries and worshipping at garish southern Indian Hindu temples.

Arriving in Medan → *Phone code: 061. Population: 2,109,030.*

Getting there

Medan is an international gateway and an easy one-hour hop by air from Singapore. There are also air connections with several Malaysian cities and many of western Indonesia's larger cities. The airport is in the centre of town. Medan's port of Belawan is visited by **PELNI** vessels that run fortnightly circuits through the Indonesian archipelago. Medan has two bus terminals. The **Amplas** terminal, 8.5 km south of the city centre, serves all destinations to the south. The **Pinang Baris** terminal, about 9 km to the northwest, serves destinations north of Medan. The train system is running, but services are limited. ➤➤ *See Transport, page 28.*

Getting around

Becak, sudaco, mesin becak (motorized becak), bis damri, metered taxi, unmetered taxi and kijang – if it moves, it can be hired. The fare around town on an oplet (minibus) is 3000Rp. For a ride on a becak expect to pay a minimum of 5000Rp; with a bit of bargaining, taxis are often available for the same price as a becak; on a mesin becak, 5000Rp. Becaks can be chartered for about 25,000Rp per hour.

Medan is a nightmare to get around; many of the main access roads are choked with traffic and the one-way system only seems to add to the frustration. However, becak drivers and taxis have become adept at chicken footing down side lanes and avoiding the main arteries.

Tourist information

The **North Sumatran Tourist Office** (Dinas Pariwisata) ⓘ *Jln Jend A Yani 107, T061 452 8436, Mon-Fri 0800-1600*, has maps and good city and regional guides. **Dinas Pariwisata** ⓘ *Jl Brig Jend Katamso 43, no telephone, daily 0900-1700*, is another tourist office but this one is less helpful and a quick peek into the visitor's book shows that around two tourists a month pop in. There is some material available but little English is spoken and it is often closed. Those who are interested in Medan's architectural heritage should try and get hold of *Tours through historical Medan and its surroundings*, by Dirk A Buiskool (1995). The pamphlet is sold in some hotel gift shops and is also available in the Dutch original.

Tours Tour companies have offices in most of the larger hotels and organize half-day city tours, and day tours to Berastagi and to the orang-utans at Bukit Lawang. Longer overnight tours to Danau Toba and to the Nias Islands are also offered by most tour agents.

Places in Medan → *For listings, see pages 25-30.*

Colonial buildings

The greatest concentration of colonial buildings is to be found along Jalan Balai Kota and its continuation, Jalan Jend A Yani, and around Merdeka Square. Few still perform their original functions as the headquarters of plantation companies, European clubs, and stately hotels. As Dirk A Buiskool explains in his pamphlet *Tours through historical Medan and its surroundings* (1995), from which much of the information below is taken, Medan underwent a building explosion during the first decade of the 20th century. The city's wealth and economic importance demanded many new buildings, and as these had to be constructed quickly there was a tendency towards standardization of design – producing what became known as 'normal architecture'.

Walking south from the northwest corner of the 'Esplanade', now **Merdeka Square** (Independence Square), the first building of note is the **Central Post Office** at Jalan Bukit Barisan 1. It was begun in 1909 and completed in 1911 and is refreshingly unchanged. Inside, the main circular hall beneath the domed roof still contains its original post office

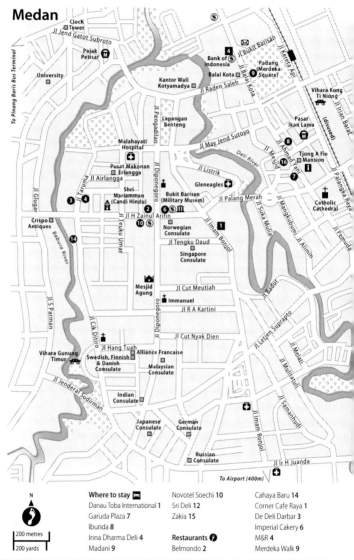

Medan

Where to stay 🛏

Danau Toba International **1**
Garuda Plaza **7**
Ibunda **8**
Inna Dharma Deli **4**
Madani **9**

Novotel Soechi **10**
Sri Deli **12**
Zakia **15**

Restaurants 🍴

Belmondo **2**

Cahaya Baru **14**
Corner Cafe Raya **1**
De Deli Darbar **3**
Imperial Cakery **6**
M&R **4**
Merdeka Walk **9**

N

200 metres
200 yards

counters. On the other side of the road was Medan's most stately hotel, the **Dharma Deli**. Today, a new block so dominates the site that the original hostelry is all but invisible. The Dharma Deli was formerly the Hotel De Boer and began life in 1898 as a modest place with just seven rooms. However, as Medan's economic influence grew, so the Hotel De Boer also expanded and by 1930 it had 120 rooms. Among the innovations introduced at the hotel was the so-called 'mosquito-less room': rooms where the windows were entirely enclosed in wire gauze, allowing people to sleep without mosquito nets. Perhaps the most famous person to have stayed at the hotel was the spy, Mata Hari.

The **Padang** itself is notable for its huge, epiphyte-filled trees that skirt the square and provide relief from the sun. On the west side of the square are two more elegant buildings, side by side: the appropriately stolid Bank of Indonesia and the refined Balai Kota. The **Bank of Indonesia**, formerly the De Javasche Bank, was designed by Ed Cuypers in 1910 in Classical style. The **Balai Kota** was probably erected in 1908 and then modernized in 1923. The clock in the elegant tower was donated by Medan's most influential Chinese businessman – Tjong A Fie (see below). The new Balai Kota, or more fully the Kantor Wali Kotyamadya, is just over the river on Jalan Raden Saleh. The architect of this building has drawn on the original Balai Kota for inspiration, most obviously in the domed tower which imitates the original, barring the blank space where the clock should be.

The Chinese community
The strip of buildings running the length of Jalan Jend A Yani from Merdeka Square south to Jalan Pemuda are very different to the buildings on the Padang; the latter is representative of the colonial government and the economic interests that sustained and supported it. These, however, were largely owned by Medan's Chinese business community – they are small **Sino-Dutch shophouses** where families would at the same time run their businesses and live, sleep and eat. Although many are marred by modern facades, they are

RM Famili **5**
Rosvin **7**
Simpang Tiga **8**
Sun Plaza **10**
Tip Top **16**

nonetheless notable for their use of both Dutch and Chinese architectural flourishes and for their variety. Most notable of all is the run-down and romantically decrepit **Tjong A Fie Mansion** at Jalan Jend A Yani 105. This quasi-colonial/quasi-Chinese house, with its green-and-beige paint scheme and peacock-topped entrance arch, was built by a wealthy Chinese businessman, after which it is named. Like other Chinese who found their fortunes in Southeast Asia, Tjong A Fie arrived in Medan from Guangdong (Canton) in 1875 almost penniless – he reputedly had a few pieces of silver sewn behind his belt. In Medan he gained the trust of the Dutch authorities and the sultan, and became the supplier for many of the area's plantations. Before long he was a millionaire and Medan's 'Major' – the highest ranking member of the Chinese community. He was a great philanthropist, giving generously to good causes – a founder, for example, of the Colonial Institute (now the Tropical Institute) in Amsterdam.

Opposite the mansion is the side street Jalan Jend A Yani I, which has a little reminder of the early days of independence in the spelling of the road name: DJln Djenderal A Yani. Walking north towards Merdeka Square a short distance is the **Tip Top Restaurant**, which began serving food and drinks in 1934 and continues to do so in a style redolent of the colonial period. Just across the railway line at the end of Jalan Jend A Yani V is the **Vihara Kong Ti Niong** – Medan's oldest Chinese pagoda.

Temples, pogodas and mosques

Another road with historical buildings is the garden-like Jalan Jend Sudirman (Polonia quarter), southwest of the town square. At the southwest edge of the city is the **Vihara Gunung Timur** ① *Jln Hang Tuah 16, photography is not allowed in the pagoda, remember to remove your shoes before entering the inner sanctuary*, just west of Jalan Cik Ditiro. This building, erected in the late 1970s, is the largest Chinese pagoda in Medan. Set in a peaceful area, the main entrance to the temple is flanked by guardian lions. Filled with lanterns, incense and demons, the temple is a rewarding retreat from the bustle of the city. The highly decorated roof is probably its most notable feature. Locally known as **Candi Hindu** (Hindu temple), the Shri Mariamman is at Jalan H Zainul Arifin 130. The complex serves Medan's large South Asian community and the brightly painted figures of gods and animals stand out a mile. The temple welcomes visitors. This part of town, reasonably enough, is the Indian quarter and the temple has been recently renovated and expanded. However, there has been a Hindu temple on the site from 1884. The **Immanuel Protestant Church**, built in 1921 in art deco style, can be found back towards the town centre at Jalan Diponegoro 25. Almost facing it on the other side of the road is the **Mesjid Agung**, with a towering new minaret.

The attractive **Mesjid Raya** or **Grand Mosque** ① *admission by donation*, with its fine black domes and turquoise tiles, can be found at the corner of Jalan Sisingamangaraja and Jalan Mesjid Raya. The mosque was built in 1906 in 'Moroccan' style by Sultan Makmun Al-Rasyid, and designed by the Dutch architect Dingemans. The marble came from Italy, the chandelier from Amsterdam, and the stained-glass from China. In the grounds is a small plot containing the tombs of the sultans of the Istana Maimun Palace, and a fairy-tale style minaret. It is a shame that the mosque is on such a busy road – it detracts from its beauty.

To the west of the mosque, set back from the road on Jalan Brig Jen Katamso, is the **Istana Maimun** – also known as the **Istana Sultan Deli** ① *daily 0800-1700, 3000Rp*. This impressive building was designed by Captain Theo van Erp, a Dutch architect working for the Royal Dutch Indies Army. It was constructed in 1888 as one element in a complex that included the Grand Mosque. The predominant colour is yellow – the colour of the royal house of Deli. It is eclectic architecturally, embracing Italian, Arab and Oriental styles. Inside are photographs of the various sultans and their wives, and a poor oil painting of the Sultan Deli himself who built the palace. The interior includes a few pieces of Dutch furniture and the sultan's throne. His descendants continue to live in one wing of the palace.

Museums and the zoo

The **Museum Sumatera Utara** ⓘ *Jln HM Joni 51, T061 771 6792, Tue-Sun 0830-1200, 1330-1700, 1000Rp*, some distance south of town off Jalan Sisingamangaraja, is an extensive building with an equally extensive – though of variable quality – collection of artefacts. Not surprisingly, it specializes in those of North Sumatran origin and upstairs has some fine wood and stone carvings from the Nias Islands. Unfortunately it is ill-lit and poorly maintained, with little useful explanatory detail. The **Bukit Barisan Museum** ⓘ *Jln H Zainul Arifin 8, T061 453 6927, Mon-Fri 0800-1500, admission by donation*, also known as the Museum Perjuangan Abri or the Military Museum, displays a decaying selection of Sumatran tribal houses and arts and crafts, as well as military paraphernalia.

Medan listings

For hotel and restaurant price codes and other relevant information, see pages 8-10.

Where to stay

Medan *p20, map p22*
The rock-bottom budget digs in Medan are no great shakes, but there are some good options in the slightly more expensive categories. There is a cluster of hotels on Jln SM Raja (Jln Sisingmangaraja), which is the best area to have a wander and compare prices.

$$$$-$$$ Novotel Soechi, Jln Cirebon 76, T061 456 1234, www.accorhotels.com/asia. This place is crawling with business people, and is deservedly popular for its excellent service, good facilities and spacious smart rooms (some with pool views). Pool, fitness centre. Free Wi-Fi in rooms. Excellent discounts available. Recommended.

$$$$-$$ Danau Toba International, Jln Imam Bonjol 17, T061 415 7000. Sprawling hotel with long list of facilities, including tennis courts and a large pool set in a garden with plenty of outdoors seating. The rooms are a tad antiquated, but comfortable, and some have garden views. Wi-Fi is available in the lobby.

$$$-$$ Hotel Garuda Plaza, Jln SM Raja 18, T061 736 1111. Large hotel with friendly staff, comfortable rooms (some with free Wi-Fi access), cable TV and complimentary newspapers. There is a pool out the back with a pleasant lounging area.

$$$-$$ Hotel Inna Dharma Deli, Jln Balai Kota 2, T061 415 7744, www.innahotels.com. This historical hotel is looking a little rough around the edges nowadays. The rooms are ultra clean, spacious and have cable TV. Free Wi-Fi is available for guests in the hotel café. Pool.

$$$-$$ Madani Hotel, Jln SM Raja 1, T061 735 8000, www.madanihotelmedan.com. There are plenty of Islamic vibes at this plush 4-star hotel, with corridors filled with Lebanese music and cafés without beer. The staff are friendly and the rooms are spotless and clean with cable TV (most foreign language channels are in Arabic). There is a 25% discount available, making this place excellent value. Recommended.

$$ Dhaksina Hotel, Jln SM Raja 20, T061 732 0000. Garish hotel with a fair selection of clean a/c rooms, although many have no windows. 10% discount available.

$$ Hotel Sumatra, Jln SM Raja 35, T061 732 1551. Big a/c rooms with clean attached bathroom, TV and some with balcony. Staff are friendly. Discounts available for stays of 5 nights or more.

$$-$ Hotel Sri Deli, Jln SM Raja 30, T061 736 8387. Good selection of rooms, including windowless economy rooms with mandi. Things get better as prices rise, with cleanish standard a/c rooms filled with light.

$$-$ Ibunda Hotel, Jln SM Raja 31-33, T061 736 8787, www.ibundahotel.com. The pea-green facade of the Ibunda is unmissable, and the colour theme continues in the interior, with its confusing staircases reminiscent of an Escher painting. The rooms here are good value, the more expensive ones are huge, and the standard singles, though a little dark, come with a/c and TV. Recommended.

$ Hotel Zakia, Jln Sipiso Piso 10-12, T061 732 2413. Staff are half conscious, but rooms here are not too bad for the price, with spartan fan rooms on the 2nd storey with veranda overlooking a small garden.

❼ Restaurants

Medan *p20, map p22*
Medan's large Chinese community means that the Chinese food here is excellent. There are many small eating houses in the street running off Jln Jend A Yani. The Indian area of town is centred on Jln Cik Ditiro and Jln H Zainal Arifin, close to Sri Mariamman Temple.

$$ Belmondo, Jln Zainul Arifin 122, T061 451 8846. Restaurant with sophisticated pretences popular with expats and locals at weekends. There is a good wine list, fusion food, seafood and a convivial atmosphere. Live jazz on Sat nights from 2000.

$$ De Deli Darbar, Jln Taruma 88, T061 415 6858. Open 1100-2230. There is plenty of choice here, with a menu that features both southern Indian veg and non-veg frontier dishes. Good selection of naan bread and tasty tidbits. Recommended.

$$ M&R, Jln Taruma 37, T061 453 6537. Daily 1100-1500 and 1800-2100. Tidy eatery furnished in traditional eastern Chinese style with caged song birds hanging from the ceiling, patrons come to sample *nyonya* (Straits Chinese fusion of Malay and Chinese flavours thought to have originated in Melaka, Malaysia) cuisine. The menu is heavy on seafood, with good crab dishes.

$$-$ Merdeka Walk, Jln Balai Kota (on the western side of Merdeka Square). Daily 1200-2400. Collection of eateries including Oh La La (bakery serving filled croissants, lasagne and cakes), Killiney Kopitiam (Singaporean franchise offering *kaya* toast, half cooked eggs and plenty of coffee), as well as some smaller stalls serving Indonesian staples.

$$-$ Sun Plaza, Jln Zainul Arifin 7, T061 450 1500. Daily 1000-2200. Shopping mall with plenty of places to eat in clean, a/c comfort. Dome and De'Excelso are cafés serving sandwiches, pastas, salads and a wide range of coffees and ice cream. Ya Kun Kaya Toast is a Singaporean outfit serving *kaya* toast (*kaya* is a rich jam made from coconut), thick coffee and half-cooked eggs. There is also an excellent food court, and branches of Bread Talk and Papa Ron's Pizza. A reassuring spot for those that have returned from jungle treks.

$ Cahaya Baru, Jln Teuku Cip Ditiro 12, T061 453 0962. Daily 1000-2200. Cheap vegetarian and non-vegetarian Indian cuisine in a clean setting. The menu features biryanis, tasty veg thalis and all the usual favourites at very sensible prices.

$ Corner Café Raya, Jln Sipiso Piso 1, T061 734 4485. Open 24 hrs. English teachers pop in here for the city's coldest beer and roast chicken and mashed potato with gravy served up in a merry ambience.

$ Imperial Cakery, Jln Zainul Arifin 116. T061 451 6230. Daily 1000-2200. Spotless bakery with good range of cakes, also serves simple pasta dishes and good sandwiches. The smoked salmon with scrambled egg on French brioche gets the day off to a good start.

$ RM Famili, Jln S M Raja, T061 736 8787.
Open 24 hrs. On the ground floor of the
Ibunda Hotel, this clean *rumah makan*
has some fine *nasi Padang* dishes, good
Malay fare including *Ikan asam pedas* (fish
cooked in a spicy tamarind sauce) and
simple Indonesian favourites. The *sirsak*
(soursop) juice here is a tropical delight.
Recommended.
$ Rosvin, Jln Ahmad Yani 114, T061
7786 0446. Small eatery serving up
a good range of spicy Acehnese and
Malay dishes, including their signature
nasi lemak (rice cooked in coconut milk
with small side dishes).
$ Simpang Tiga, Jln Ahmad Yani 83, T061
453 6721. Glorious *nasi Padang* (spicy West
Sumatran food) in full a/c comfort as well
as a play area for kids.
$ Tip Top, Jln Ahmad Yani 92, T061 451
4442. Daily 0800-2200. The venue of choice
for the city's older generation of Chinese-
Indonesians for a morning coffee and a
chat, the Tip Top has pleasant outdoor
seating, plenty of ice cream, a touch of
colonial decadence and distinctly average
Indonesian and Chinese dishes.

🎵 Bars and clubs

Medan *p20, map p22*
Most hotels in the upper categories have
bars, which stay open until around 0200.
Hotel Danau Toba International
(see Where to stay). Has 5 venues for
boozing, including Dangdut International
(with, unsurprisingly, live *dangdut* –
Indonesian pop music heavily influenced
by Bollywood and Arabic music), Rock Café
and Tobasa Club with its different theme
evenings including Ladies' Night on Thu
and DJs at the weekend.
Zodiac, at the Novotel Soechi (see Where
to stay). Live music at weekends, and some
good drinks promotions.

🎬 Entertainment

Medan *p20, map p22*
Cinema
There is a cinema on the 3rd floor of
the Grand Palladium (see Shopping)
showing all the latest blockbusters,
and some Indonesian films (20,000Rp).
For information on what is currently
showing, phone T061 451 4321.

❂ Festivals

Medan *p20, map p22*
Idul Fitri (Islamic holy day), is a movable
feast. Muslims descend on the Maimun
Palace in traditional dress to mark the end
of the fasting month of Ramadan – a very
colourful occasion.
Mar-May Medan Fair is held each year
at the Taman Ria Amusement Park on Jln
Gatot Subroto. There are also permanent
cultural exhibits at the park.

❂ Shopping

Medan *p20, map p22*
Antiques Jln Jend A Yani is the
main shopping area, with the largest
concentration of 'antique' shops. Beware
of fakes: old Batak artefacts are cunningly
mass produced and there are few real
antiques for sale these days.

Books There is a branch of Gramedia
at the Sun Plaza (see below) with a small
selection of English-language books and
magazines such as *Time* and *The Economist*.

Malls Sun Plaza, Jln Zainul Arifin 7, T061
450 1500, daily 1000-2200, has clothes
shops, opticians, computer hardware and
software and restaurants; Grand Palladium,
Jln Kapten Mohlan Lubis 8, T061 451 4939,
daily 0900-2200, cinema, mobile phones,
magazines, (a few English language titles)
and a huge supermarket in the basement.

Markets One of the greatest attractions of Medan is its markets, known locally as *pajak*. The huge **Pajak Pusat** (Central Market) – in fact an agglomeration of various markets selling just about everything – is located close to Jalan Dr Sutomo. It is renowned for its pickpockets. Safer is the **Pajak Petisar**, on Jln Rasak Baru, just off Jln Gatot Subroto. It is a fruit and vegetable market in the morning (0600), that later develops into a general market, selling clothes, food and general merchandise. The **Pasar (Pajak) Ikan Lama** (Old Fish Market) is a good place to buy cheap batik, other types of cloth and assorted garments. It is on Jalan Perniagaan, close to Jln Jend A Yani. Visitors may see live fruit bats strung up for sale.

Supermarkets Kedai 24, Jln SM Raja, located near the hotels, open 24 hrs, has most daily necessities. If you can't find what you need here, then head to the top floor of **Yuki Simpang Raya**, opposite the Mesjid Raya, which has a slightly more comprehensive selection.

Textiles Jln Jend A Yani III, which runs off Jln Jend A Yani, has a number of textile outlets. Browsing through the markets can be rewarding – either the massive **Central Market** or the **Old Fish Market**; the latter is the best place to buy batik (see Markets, above). Formal batik can be found at **Batik Danar Hadi**, Jln Zainul Arifin 117, T061 457 4273, daily 0900-2100.

⚙ What to do

Medan *p20, map p22*
Tour operators
There are travel and tour companies all over town and most will provide a range of services from booking airline tickets through to providing tours and bus tickets. There is a concentration along Jln Katamso, south of the intersection with Jln Letjen Suprapto.

Amalia Amanda Tour and Travel, Jln Katamso 43, T061 452 1666. Ferry tickets to Penang.
Erni Tour, Jln Katamso 43 J, T061 456 4666. Ticketing and money changer.
Mutiara Tour and Travel, Jln Katamso 43 K, T061 456 6700. Ferry tickets and flights to Malaysia.
Perdana Ekspres, Jln Katamso 35C, T061 456 6222. Penang ferry tickets and PELNI agent.
Tobali Tour, Jln SM Raja 79, T061 732 4472. Tourist buses to Danau Toba.
Trophy Tour, Jln Katamso 33, T061 415 5777, www.trophytour.com. International and domestic ticketing. Very well established.

⊖ Transport

Medan *p20, map p22*
Air
Medan's **Polonia International Airport** is 3 km south of the town – effectively within the city. A taxi from the city centre to the airport costs 20,000Rp. Or take a bus from Pinang Baris terminal (in the direction of Amplas terminal) and get off at the traffic lights on Jln Juanda, the airport is 500 m on the right (3000Rp). There is a fixed-price taxi booth in the airport, on the right just before the exit. The fare to Jln SM Raja is a steep 35,000Rp.

Domestic To **Banda Aceh** daily with Sriwijaya, Garuda Indonesia and Kartika; **Pekanbaru** daily with Sriwijaya; **Padang** daily with Mandala; **Batam** daily with Lion Air and Sriwijaya; **Padang** daily with Mandala and Lion Air; **Yogyakarta** daily via **Padang** with Mandala; **Jakarta** daily with Garuda, AirAsia, Lion Air and Sriwijjaya.

International Daily to **Singapore** with Singapore Airlines and regular connections on **Jetstar Asia** (www.jetstar.com). AirAsia has daily flights to **Kuala Lumpur**. Also daily direct flights to **Penang** with AirAsia, Lion Air and Kartika Airlines.

Boat

Medan's port, **Belawan**, is 26 km north of the city. Shuttle buses meet passengers from the ferry. The fare into town is 9000Rp. However, ferry companies provide transport to Belawan from their offices as part of the cost of the ticket to **Penang**. Town buses for Belawan leave from the intersection of Jln Balai Kota and Jln Guru Patimpus, near the TVRI offices. Oplets also travel to Belawan (the destination is displayed). The **PELNI** vessels *Kelud* and *Sinabung* call into Belawan on their way to Jakarta's Tanjung Priok. Of most use to travellers is the *Sinabung*, which stops at **Batam** (30-min ferry ride from Singapore), before heading to **Java**. This vessel departs every Tue. Check the latest PELNI schedule at the booking agent **Perdana Ekspres**, Jln Katamso 35C, T061 4566 2222.

Various companies run ferries: **Perdana Ekspres**, Jln Katamso 35C, T061 456 6222, and their partner **Amalia Amanda**, Jln Katamso 43, T061 452 1666, have express boats to **Penang** sailing Tue, Thu, Sat at 1000. The journey takes 5-6 hrs. The one-way fare is US\$36 plus US\$3 seaport tax. The return fare is US\$60 plus US\$3 seaport tax. Transport to **Belawan** is provided free by the company, but the trip from Belawan to **Medan** is charged at 9000Rp. **Perdana Ekspres** has an office in Penang at Ground Floor PPC Building, Pesara King Edward, T04 262 0802. Ferries leave **Penang** Mon, Wed, Fri at 0900. Fares are the same. Tickets can also be booked at www.langkawi-ferry.com.

Bus

Medan has 2 main bus terminals: Amplas and Pinang Baris. **Amplas terminal** is on Jln Medan Tenggara VII, 8.5 km south of the city centre off Jln Sisingamangaraja, and serves all destinations south of Medan including **Bukittinggi**, **Parapat** and **Danau Toba** (6 hrs, 25,000Rp), **Jakarta**, **Bali**, **Jambi**, **Dumai**, **Pekanbaru**, **Palembang** and **Sibolga**. Get there by yellow oplet running south (Nos 24, 52 or 57), 3000Rp. Major bus companies like **ALS** have their offices on Jln Sisingamangaraja close to the terminal (at the 6.5 km marker). The most comfortable way of getting to **Danau Toba** is to take the tourist minibus service offered by **Tobali Tour**, Jln SM Raja 79C, T061 732 4472, for 80,000Rp. The bus departs at 0900. Phone ahead to book a seat and ask to be picked up at your hotel.

The **Pinang Baris terminal** is on Jln Pinang Baris (off Jln Gatot Subroto, which becomes Jln Binjei), about 9 km northwest of the city centre, and serves **Banda Aceh** and other destinations north of Medan including **Bukit Lawang** (leaving every 30 mins, 3 hrs, 15,000Rp – don't pay the touts who wait for tourists, pay the driver at the end of your journey); and **Berastagi**, 2 hrs, 7000Rp. Get to the terminal by orange or green microlet running along Jln Gatot Subroto. The best way of getting to Berastagi is to catch microlet No 41 from the front of Yuki Simpang Raya heading to **Padang Bulan**, 3000Rp. Tell the driver you want to get off at Simpang Pos, where the streets are lined with buses heading to Berastagi and **Kebonjahe**, 2 hrs, 7000Rp. **Jakarta**, US\$38; **Yogyakarta**, US\$40; **Padang** and **Bukittinggi**, 20-22 hrs, US\$14 or a/c US\$24.

Bus companies It makes sense to book a seat over the phone rather than traipsing all the way to the offices the day before departure. Your hotel should be able to help you. **Pelangi**, Jln Gajah Mada 56, T061 457011, runs to Pekanbaru, Palembang, Banda Aceh and Jakarta. **PMTOH**, Jln Gajah Mada 57, T061 415 2546, serves **Banda Aceh**, **Yogya**, **Solo**, **Jakarta**. ANS, Jln SM Raja 30, T061 786 0667, super executive buses to Jakarta, Bukittinggi, Padang and Bandung. ALS, Jln SM Raja Km6.5, T061 786685, has services to Dumai (for ferries to Batam and for Melaka, Malaysia), Jakarta, Banda Aceh, Yogya and Solo.

Car hire

National Car Rental, Hotel Inna Dharma Deli, see Where to stay. Cars with driver can be rented from the **Sri Deli Hotel**, see Where to stay.

Taxi

Can be rented by the day; ask at your hotel. Fares within Medan range from 10,000Rp to 25,000Rp (more if buying from the fixed-price booth at the airport). Most taxi companies are located at Jln Sisingamangaraja 60-107.

Train

The station is on Jln Prof M Yamin. The schedule from the train station is a little erratic. There are a couple of daily departures to **Rantau Parapat** (4-5 hrs, 55,000Rp/75,000Rp). Check the latest schedule at the station.

● Directory

Medan *p20, map p22*
Banks If travelling from Penang to Medan via Belawan Port, it is advisable to change money in Georgetown (Penang) before departure – the exchange rate is much better than in Medan. There are numerous banks in Medan, all fairly internationally minded. **Duta Bank** offers cash advances against Visa and MasterCard. The **Hong Kong Bank** has a 24-hr ATM. There are also a number of money changers on Jln Katamso. **Bank Central Asia**, Jln Bukit Barisan 3, will provide cash advances on

Visa). **Bank Dagang Negara**, Jln JendA Yani 109. **Duta Bank**, Jln Sisingamangaraja, next to the Garuda Plaza Hotel. **Ekspor Impor (Bank Exim)**, Jln Balai Kota 8. **Bank Negara Indonesia**, Jln Jend A Yani 72. **Standard Chartered Bank**, Jln Imam Bonjol 17, T061 453 8800. Money changers include: **King's Money Changer**, Jln Pemuda 24; and **PT Supra**, Jln Jend A Yani 101. **Embassies and consulates** For Indonesian embassies and consulates abroad and for foreign embassies in Indonesia, see http://embassy.goabroad.com.
Immigration Jln Binjai Km 6.2, T061 451 2112. **Internet** Most tourists head to the efficient internet café in the basement of Yukji Simpang Raya department store on Jln Sisingamangaraja. There are also facilities at the **Novotel Soechi Medan** and the **Central Post Office**. **Medical services** Bunda Clinic (open 24 hrs), Jln Sisingamangaraja, T061 7032 1666; **Herna Hospital**, Jln Majapahit 118A, T061 414 7715; **Gleneagles Hospital**, Jln Listrik 6, T061 456 6268, is reputed to be the best in town. **Police** Jln Durian, T061 452 0453. **Post office** Central Post Office, Jln Bukit Barisan 1 (on Merdeka Sq). **Telephone** At the **General Post Office**, Jln Bukit Barisan 1 (at Central Post Office) for overseas calls. There are other **Wartel** offices all over town, including on Jln Sisingamangaraja (next to the Hotel Deli Raya and opposite the Mesjid Raya) and on Jln Irian Barat (just north of the intersection with Jln Let Jend MT Haryono). Calls can also be placed from the **Tip Top Café** on Jln Jend A Yani.

Bukit Lawang

Bukit Lawang, sometimes also named 'Gateway to the Hills', is a small community on the edge of the Gunung Leuser Nature Reserve, an area of beautiful countryside. A few years ago Bukit Lawang was a thriving place with thousands of tourists coming to see the orang-utans. This is no longer true. The downturn in tourism in Indonesia has hit Sumatra hard. Things got worse for the town in November 2003 when a flash food swept away much of the infrastructure and killed hundreds of residents. However, there is a real sense of resilience and community here, and the people are working hard to get the town firmly back on the tourist trail. Visitors will note the effort made to keep the area clean, with recycling and rubbish bins along all the paths in the village.

Arriving in Bukit Lawant → *Phone code: 061.*

Getting there

Direct buses leave from Medan's Pinang Baris terminal every 30 minutes (three hours, 15,000Rp). From Berastagi catch a bus to Medan and get off at Pinang Baris; from here, catch a regular bus to Bukit Lawang. Taxis can be hired in Medan, the journey will take two hours.➡ *See Transport, page 35.*

Tourist information

The **Visitor Information Centre** ⓘ *daily 0700-1500*, has free maps and can offer advice on hiking. It also sells a useful booklet on the park and its wildlife and flora (12,000Rp). You can get park permits here, including long-term research permits.

For free maps and a price list of guided tours, contact the guides association, **HPI** ⓘ *opposite the Visitor Information Centre, T081 3707 30151, daily 0800-1500.*

Orang-Utan Rehabilitation Centre

Just outside the village is the famous centre established in 1973 – now one of Sumatra's most popular tourist destinations. The work of the centre is almost entirely supported by revenue from tourism. The orang-utan (*Pongo pygmaeus*) is on the verge of extinction throughout its limited range across island Southeast Asia, and the centre has been established by the Worldwide Fund for Nature to rehabilitate domesticated orang-utans for life in the wild. The problem is that there is a ready black market for orang-utans as pets and in Medan they sell for US$350. However, when the young, friendly animals grow up into powerful, obstreperous adult apes, they are often abandoned and some end up at Bukit Lawang. Locals come from Medan to frolic in the river, not to see the apes, so while the river may be busy, feeding time is comparatively quiet.

Getting there

The entrance to the reserve is a 30-minute walk from the village, following the Bohorok River upstream, which then has to be crossed by boat; from there it is another 20 minutes or so up

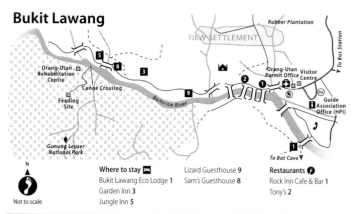

Bukit Lawang

Not to scale

Where to stay ⬛	Lizard Guesthouse 9	Restaurants ⓐ
Bukit Lawang Eco Lodge 1	Sam's Guesthouse 8	Rock Inn Cafe & Bar 1
Garden Inn 3		Tony's 2
Jungle Inn 5		

a steepish path to the feeding point. Alternatively, buses and minibuses travel down Jalan Gatot Subroto, which becomes Jalan Binjei, leaving from the Central Market (45 minutes, 3000Rp). Leave Bukit Lawang an hour before feeding time to allow for the journey.

Entry to the park
Visitors can see the apes during feeding times (0800-0900 and 1500-1600, you should aim to get there five minutes beforehand). The times do sometimes change, so check at the PHKA office in Bukit Lawang. Guides can be hired from the PHKA office for one-, two- or three-day treks of varying difficulty and visitors have reported seeing gibbons, monkeys and orang-utans. All visitors must obtain a permit from the PHKA office (one day: 20,000Rp, plus 50,000Rp for camera and 150,000Rp for video camera) before entering the park. A passport must be shown before a permit is issued (although this is not strictly enforced). Afternoons are more crowded, especially at weekends; it is best to stay the night and watch a morning, weekday, feed if possible.

Next door to the PHPA office is a **Visitor Information Centre** ① *daily 0700-1500, donation requested*, which shows films in English on Monday and Friday at 2000 (when equipment is working), and also has a study room and a display.

Around Bukit Lawang

There are a number of caves in the vicinity. For the **Bat Cave** ① *5000Rp*, take a torch and non-slip shoes; it is not an easy climb and a guide is recommended (10,000Rp). There is also a **rubber processing plant** close by – ask at the visitors centre for a handout and map.

Tubing
Floating down the Bohorok River on an inner tube has become a popular excursion. Tubes can be hired for 10,000Rp per day in the village for the 12 km (two to three hours) journey to the first bridge. There is public transport from the bridge back to Bukit Lawang. For US$50 you can trek upstream and return in the late afternoon by inner tube. Dry bags are provided for cameras and other valuables. Beware of whirlpools and watch out for low branches; tourists have drowned in the past.

Hiking
Hiking is the best way to experience the forest and see the wildlife. The visitor centre has handouts and maps of hiking trails and guesthouses, and may be able to provide information about guides for jungle treks. Head to the Association of Indonesian Guides, HPI ① *near the visitor centre, T081 3707 30151, daily 0800-1500*, for a map, price list for treks and other information. Bukit Lawang has more than 130 guides, massively outnumbering the tourists and so there is some pressure to take one. The HPI office recommends getting a guide directly from their office, where they can match a guide to your interests and ensure the correct price. Note that all official guides carry an HPI identity card. Languages include English, German, Spanish, French and Dutch. Prices for all hikes are fixed by the HPI office. A three-hour hike costs US$22, one-day hike US$36 (plus US$14 to tube down the river back to Bukit Lawang after the trek), two days for US$80 (plus US$14 for tubing) and three days for US$100. All prices include guide, transportation, permit, food and tent.

It is possible to hike to **Berastagi** in three days at a cost of US$118. This trek is less popular because so much of the route has been deforested. Instead, those visitors wishing to trek through true jungle should opt for the five- to seven-day hike to **Kutacane**, US$300. Most treks require a minimum of three to four people. Note that these are arduous treks requiring fitness and hiking boots; check the credentials of guides – many lack experience (they should be able to produce a legal licence and permit). During the rainy season (around August-December) there can be very heavy downpours and good waterproofs are essential.

Whitewater rafting
The HPI offer rafting trips on the nearby Wampu River, costing around US$60 per person per day. These are sometimes combined with a trek.

Tangkahan → For listings, see pages 34-35.

Tangkahan lies about 40 km north of Bukit Lawang, next to the Gunung Leuser National Park and there is only one resort here, the **Bamboo River Guesthouse** (see Where to stay, page 35). What is special about this place is its proximity to unspoilt lowland rainforest, and the absence of tourists. No trekking is promoted here, so bird and animal life is more active. It is possible to hike (guide strongly recommended), take a canoe trip down the Batang Serangan River, or visit some hot sulphur springs.

Getting there
Tangkahan is a five-hour chartered bus ride from Bukit Lawang, ask at the tourist office for more information. From Medan, catch a bus from the Pinang Baris terminal to Tangkahan (three hours). At the river crossing in Tangkahan, shout for the raft man.

Bukit Lawang listings

For hotel and restaurant price codes and other relevant information, see pages 8-10.

🛏 Where to stay

Bukit Lawang *p31, map p32*
The road ends at the bus stop, so reaching guesthouses further upstream means as much as a 25-min slog on foot. About 15 or so *losmen* line the Bohorok River up to the crossing-point for the reserve. Many guesthouses were damaged by the flood in 2003, and some were forced out of business. The slowdown means it is easy to find somewhere to sleep. The views and jungle atmosphere are best upriver, towards the park entrance.

A recent venture being organized through the Visitor Information Centre involves camping on the edge of the national park, a 2-hr walk from the village past the Bat Cave. The campsite is on the edge of a river and is very secluded. A great way to escape the crowds and witness nature first-hand. Enquire at the HPI office. There are currently no tents available to rent.
$$-$ Bukit Lawang Eco Lodge, T081 2607 9983. Set in lovely gardens, which produce some tasty vegetables for evening meals. With plenty of eco-friendly ideals, this hotel is one of the more popular places. The rooms are clean and comfortable, although don't have the views of some of the places further up the river. Recommended.
$$-$ Jungle Inn, T081 3753 24015, a.rahman3775@yahoo.co.id. The most popular guesthouse in Bukit Lawang with an extraordinary selection of rooms. The cheapest, out the back, have a balcony next to a small waterfall and gushing stream. There is one room with a rockface as a wall. The more expensive rooms are large and decadent (for Bukit Lawang) with 4-poster beds, thoughtful decoration and stunning views. The staff here are friendly, and the sunset sees guitars and bongos being taken

from their hiding places for a Sumatran sing-along. Recommended.

$ Bukit Lawang Indah Guesthouse, T081 5276 15532. 38 clean and spacious rooms with fan and squat toilet. 24-hr electricity.

$ Garden Inn, T081 3968 43235. Rickety wooden structures with perilous stairs. Rooms have balcony with sublime river views, and bathrooms with squat toilet. Recommended.

$ Jungle Tribe, T081 3751 26275. Offers 1 room, more planned. Spacious, with balcony.

$ The Lizard Guesthouse. Friendly place right on the river with simple rattan-walled rooms. The café downstairs has a TV and selection of DVDs. The owner speaks superb English and is a good source of information.

$ Sam's Guesthouse, T081 3700 93597. The rooms that have been finished are pleasant, some with beautiful views over the river and comfy beds with mosquito nets.

Tangkahan *p34*

$ Bamboo River Guesthouse, on the Buluh River, Tangkahan, 40 km north of Bukit Lawang, no telephone, communication is by walkie-talkie. Owned by an English woman and a local senior guide. Has 10 rooms and an evening meal costs around 25,000Rp.

Restaurants

Bukit Lawang *p31, map p32*
There are plenty of stalls near the bridges offering simple local fare. Most of the hotels have decent menus (all **$**).

$ Green Hill Café. Pool table and simple snacks in a breezy riverine setting.

$ The Jungle Inn. Fine potato and pumpkin curries and juices made with local honey.

$ Jungle Tribe. Macaroni cheese and pizzas somewhat overshadowed by the extensive cocktail list for those wanting a jungle party.

$ Rock Inn Café and Bar. Daily 0900-2400. Built into a rockface, with a motorbike hanging from the wall, this local hang-out offers curries, soups, tacos and spaghetti.

$ Tony's Restaurant. Daily 0700-2300. Small bamboo eatery serving up fair pizzas. The owner is proud of her fettuccine, which she says gets top marks from European visitors.

Transport

Bukit Lawang *p31, map p32*
Bus
There are no direct buses from Bukit Lawang to Berastagi. Instead head back to Pinang Baris and jump on a Berastagi-bound bus (2 hrs, 7000Rp).

Directory

Bukit Lawang *p31, map p32*
Banks *Losmen* and tour companies change money, but rates are poor so bring sufficient cash. **Post office** Some stalls sell stamps and will post letters.
Telephone Wartel office in main 'village'. Mobile reception gets poorer the further up the river you go.

Berastagi

Berastagi, is a hill resort town, lying 1400 m above sea level on the Karo Plateau among the traditional lands of the Karo Batak people. Though Berastagi may not be a one-horse town, it gives the impression of being a one-road town. There is also the distinct feel that it has become a way-station, a sort of trucking stop between other more important places.

Arriving in Berastagi → *Phone code: 0628.*

Getting there
Berastagi is 68 km from Medan and 147 km from Parapat. There are regular bus connections with Medan (two hours, 7000Rp). Getting from Parapat on a public bus is a little more complicated as it involves changes. The bus station is at the south end of the main road, Jalan Veteran. ▸ *See Transport, page 41.*

Getting around
Visitors can travel easily around town on foot, by bicycle and using oplets. For the surrounding villages and towns cars can be hired and oplets service some routes. Dokars can also be used for short local journeys; in Berastagi these are known as *sados*.

Tourist information
Staff at **Dinas Pariwisata** ⓘ *Jln Gundaling No 1, T0628 91084,* speak good English and are a useful source of local information. Their guided hikes up the nearby volcanoes are some of the cheapest in town. The **Sibayak Guesthouse** ⓘ *Jln Veteran 119,* and the **Wisma Ginsata** ⓘ *Jln Veteran 79,* are also excellent sources of information. The Sibayak keeps a particularly useful comments book.

Places in Berastagi → *For listings, see pages 39-41.*

The town does not have many specific sights of interest, but its position, surrounded by active volcanoes, is memorable. Unfortunately, Berastagi has a rather uncared-for feel, and it is somewhat featureless. Nonetheless, it is a good place to cool off after the heat and bustle of Medan, and go for a mountain hike. It is also a good base from which to explore the surrounding countryside.

For those without the time to visit the Batak villages outside Kabanjahe, there is a Batak village of sorts – **Peceren** ⓘ *2000Rp for admission to village,* just outside town on the road to Medan, 100 m past the **Rose Garden Hotel**. It is rather run down and dirty, with a few Batak houses interspersed with modern houses; however, it is in some respects more authentic than those that have been preserved, showing how living communities are adapting to the changing world. Just 200 m or so up Jalan Gundaling from here is a strange Buddhist temple – the **Vihara Buddha**. How the architect managed to arrive at this fusion of styles is not clear, but 'ungainly' would not be an unkind description. The general goods market behind the bus station is worth a wander.

Around Berastagi

Kabanjahe

ⓘ *12 km south of Berastagi. Easily accessible by bus, regular departures from the bus station on Jln Veteran, 25 mins, 3000Rp.*

Meaning 'Ginger garden', Kabanjahe lies on the main road and scores of buses and oplets make the journey. It is a local market town of some size and little charm, but it is worth visiting on Monday market day. Kabanjahe is also an important communication town. From here it is possible to walk to traditional villages of the Karo Batak people (see below).

Lingga and Barusja

ⓘ *Catch a bus from the bus station on Jln Veteran to Kabanjahe, and from there a microlite or bemo onwards; in Kabanjahe they leave from the intersection of Jln Pala Bangun, Jln Veteran and Jln Bangsi Sembiring. To visit Lingga, an 'entrance fee' of 2000Rp must be paid at the tourist information centre in the main square (visitors with a guide may not have to pay).*

Berastagi

N
Not to scale

Where to stay 🛏
Ginsata &
  Wisma Ginsata **3**
Melati Bangkit Nan Jaya **14**
Sibayak Losmen **5**
Sibayak Internasional **9**
Sibayak Multinational
  Guesthouse **10**
Wisma Sibayak **11**
Wisma Sunrise **13**

Restaurants 🍴
Eropa **1**
Mexico Fried Chicken **4**
Raymond Café **2**

Karo Batak villages are to be found dotted all over the hills around Berastagi. The more traditional villages are not accessible by road and must be reached on foot; to visit these communities it is recommended to hire a guide (ask at your hotel or the tourist centre). It can make sense to charter a bemo for the day – a lot more ground can be covered.

Two villages that can be visited with relative ease from Kabanjahe are Lingga and Barusjahe. Both can be reached by microlite from Kabanjahe. This ease of access has inevitably resulted in rather 'touristy' villages. **Lingga**, is about 4 km northwest of Kabanjahe and is a community of some 30 Batak houses, of which there are about a dozen traditional longhouses. There are overpriced carvings for sale. Photographs of the local people might require payment. **Barusjah** is slightly more difficult to get to and as a result is marginally more 'traditional', but can still be reached by microlite from Kabanjahe. It is rather a dirty village with very few houses in the traditional style, but there are a few over two centuries old (and as a result are decaying badly). The soaring roofs are particularly impressive.

Dokan

ⓘ *Catch a Simas bus at the bus terminal in Kabanjahe and ask to be set down at the Dokan turn (13 km from Kabanjahe), it is then a 3-km walk to the village, a donation is expected. Buses on to Sipisopiso are usually pretty crowded.*

Dokan is a fine Karo Batak village that lies halfway between Kabanjahe and Sipisopiso, where villagers are less inclined to hassle.

Sipisopiso waterfalls

ⓘ *24 km from Kabanjahe, a 1-hr drive southeast of Berastagi. Catch a bemo to Pemangtangsiantar and ask to get off at Simpang Sitanggaling. The falls are a 30-min walk from here or a quick ojek ride away. Entry to the falls is 2000Rp.*

The falls cascade through a narrow gap in the cliffside and then fall 120 m to **Danau Toba**. It is possible to walk along a spur to a small gazebo for a good view of the falls, or to walk to the bottom and back takes about one hour. There is the usual array of souvenir stalls and *warungs*. In spite of the commercialism, the falls are a pretty spectacular sight. There is no accommodation here, but from Sipisopiso towards **Parapat** is **Siantar Hotel**, a nice place to stop for coffee and fried bananas. In its garden and restaurant you have a superb view of the lake, but despite its name you cannot sleep there, it is only a restaurant.

Mount Sibayak

Sibayak lies northwest of Berastagi at 2095 m and can be climbed in a day, but choose a fair weather day and leave early for the best views (and to avoid the rain). Take the trail from behind Gundaling Hill, ask at your hotel for directions before setting out. Guides can be easily found (again, ask at your hotel – they will charge US$7-15 depending on the size of the party), and a map of the route is available from the **Tourist Information Office**. Information is also available from either the **Ginsata** or **Sibayak** guesthouses. Wear good walking shoes and take a sweater as it can be chilly. It takes about two to three hours to reach the summit, along a logging road, or alternatively there is a jungle trek that is quicker if you take a bemo to Semangat Gunung, in the Daulu Valley. Over the summit, the descent is down 2000 steps to reach the hot water and **Sulphur Springs** ⓘ *daily 0800-2300, 5000Rp.* The sulphur is collected by local people and is used as medicine and as a pesticide.

Mount Sinabung

Sinabung, which rises to 2454 m to the west of Berastagi, is another popular climb. There are now three routes up the volcano. One of the routes is well marked but it is best to take a guide as heavy rain and mist can make it very dangerous (see note, below). Seven people disappeared here in 1996/1997, when mist made it impossible for them to find the path. Maps are available from the Sibayak guesthouses.

To climb the mountain without a guide, catch a bus to Danau Lau Kawar (one hour, 6000Rp). The path from the village passes a restaurant; fork left just after the restaurant (do not continue along the main path). This path then passes a house and on the left you will see a small hut; you need to turn left again onto another path that passes the hut. The route then works its way through the forest for one hour and is relatively well marked with arrows and string. As the path leaves the forest it becomes very steep and enters a rock gully (also steep). The route passes an old campsite and then a cliff overhang decorated with graffiti. (This makes a good shelter in bad weather as hot steam issues through vents.) After around three to four hours in total, the path reaches the summit. Paths skirt the crater lip but care is needed.

Take good hiking boots, a jumper, a change of clothes, and a water bottle. Tents can be hired from the Sibayak guesthouses. Leeches can sometimes be a problem.

Note The Tourist Information Service recommends that visitors take a guide with them on mountain hikes as the weather is very unpredictable and the thick jungle on the flanks of the mountains leads into the massive Gunung Leuser National Park where it is very easy to get lost. The Tourist Information Service and Ginsata have a list of recent tourist mishaps on the mountain, including details of an Austrian tourist who got lost on Sibayak in 2007, and was found nine days later unconscious in a garden in a small town on the edge of the park. He claimed he was led further into the jungle by the ghosts of two German tourists, missing since 1997, a claim locals – with their appreciation of anything connected to the supernatural – seem to believe heartily.

Sidikalang

This is a small, unremarkable town, 75 km southwest of Berastagi, which serves an important 'linking' function. From here it is possible to travel north, along the valley of the Alas River to Kutacane and the Gunung Leuser National Park, and from there to Takengon and the Gayo Highlands, and finally to Banda Aceh at the northern tip of Sumatra. Alternatively, it is possible to travel west to the coast and then north along the coast, again to Banda Aceh. The countryside around here is locally known for the quality of its coffee.

Tongging

Tongging is a small town on Danau Toba's northern shore. Like the much more popular Samosir Island, it is possible to swim in the lake and generally relax, although the tourist infrastructure here is not nearly as developed. It is a good base to see the Sipisopiso falls (see above) and also a number of relatively untouristy Batak villages, including **Silalahi**. Tongging can also be used as an alternative route to Samosir – there are boats from Tongging to Samosir via Haranggaol every Monday at 0730.

Berastagi listings

For hotel and restaurant price codes and other relevant information, see pages 8-10.

● Where to stay

Berastagi *p36, map p37*
Berastagi is not a particularly attractive town, but it does have a selection of some of the best *losmen* in Sumatra. Not only are the rooms clean and well maintained, but the owners go out of their way to provide travellers with information on the surrounding area. They arrange trips to traditional ceremonies, inform travellers on the best way to climb the mountains and on hikes, and are generally highly constructive. Breakfast is not usually included in the price.

$$$$-$$$ Sibayak Internasional Hotel, Jln Merdeka, T0628 91301, www.hotel sibayak.com. A 4-star hotel perched on a hillside overlooking the town. Rooms are clean, with cable TV. There is a pool, tennis court, disco, putting green and free Wi-Fi access in the lounge area. 40% discount available.

$ Ginsata Hotel and Guesthouse, Jln Veteran 27, T0628 91441. The hotel is on the noisy main road and has clean rooms with cold-water shower. The guesthouse (enquire at hotel office) around the corner is much quieter and has tidy simple rooms. The owner is an excellent source of local information. Recommended.

$ Hotel Melati Bangkit Nan Jaya, Jln Pendidikan 82, T081 2646 5006. Relaxed place out of town, with pleasant rooms, some with TV. There is no restaurant, but they can prepare a simple evening meal on request. Bargain for a decent price.

$ Sibayak Losmen, Jln Veteran 119, T0628 91095. This *losmen* is reached by walking through a travel agent's office. One of the more homely options in town, the staff here are friendly and offer excellent information on tours. The rooms with attached bathroom (cold water, squat toilet) on the 2nd floor are clean, but some are windowless. The cheaper rooms on the top floor have shared bathroom and access to a lovely roof terrace. Hot-water showers are available for 5000Rp.

$ Sibayak Multinational Guesthouse, Jln Pendidikan 93, T0628 91031, irnawati_pelawi@yahoo.co.id. 2 km out of town on the road leading towards Gunung Sibayak, this place is set in sprawling gardens with excellent views and a quiet atmosphere. More expensive rooms are big with hot-water showers. The smaller, old-style rooms are passable, but have no hot water.

$ Wisma Sibayak, Jln Udara 1, T0628 91104, bhirinxz@yahoo.com. What looks like a Malay doll's house from the outside, is home to the best budget accommodation in town, with excellent local information, spotless rooms with or without attached bathroom (cold water), lots of communal space and friendly vibes. Recommended.

$ Wisma Sunrise, Jln Kaliaga 5, T0628 92404. Simple, clean rooms with cold-water shower. This place has superb views over the town and down to the plains beyond. The owner works at the tourist office in town and can arrange tours to Danau Toba and Bukittinggi. There are no eating facilities here.

❼ Restaurants

Berastagi *p36, map p37*
There are a good number of restaurants along Jln Veteran – serving mainly Padang food. Fruits grown in the area include avocados and *marquisa* (passion fruit); the latter is made into a delicious drink.

$ Eropa, Jln Veteran 48G, T0628 91365. Daily 0700-2100. Simple eatery with a long list of Chinese dishes and some Western dishes such as soups, pasta and steaks. Good for those needing a dose of pork.

$ Losmen Sibayak. Decent Western and Indonesian fare.

$ Mexico Fried Chicken, Jln Veteran 18, T0628 93252. Open 0800-2300. Fast-food fans might want to pop in. The entrance has a sign with a Hispanic man wearing a panama hat with MFC emblazoned on it. Fried chicken set meals, burgers and coffee form the menu.

$ Raymond Café, Jln Trimurti, T0813 9742 8979. Daily 0700-2300. Friendly and a good place to meet travellers, chat with locals and get a taste of the delicious local vegetables. The avocado salad with a lemon juice dressing is superb, as are the juices. Simple Western and Indonesian fare is good value here. Recommended.

$ Wisma Sibayak. Serves traveller-friendly Western and Indonesian fare.

Foodstalls

There are many open-air *warungs* serving good, fresh food, using the temperate fruit and vegetables grown in the surrounding countryside. **Jln Veteran** has the best selection. The market near the monument just off Jln Veteran sells fresh produce.

❻ Shopping

Berastagi *p36, map p37*
Antiques and handicrafts Sold in several shops along Jln Veteran. **Mamaken** at Jln Veteran 16, T0628 91256, daily 0800-2100, sell mostly Batak pieces.

❹ What to do

Berastagi *p36, map p37*
Hiking
It is possible to hike through spectacular countryside, all the way to Bukit Lawang

from Berastagi in 3 days. However, the government is anxious about visitors disturbing this culturally sensitive area and trekkers should take the time and care to organize trips properly. Ask in town at the Sibayak Guesthouse or at the Tourist Information Service, Jln Gundaling 1, for trekking information. There are numerous guides offering treks to Bukit Lawang; this is a difficult and demanding trek requiring a degree of fitness and good walking boots. Most people trek this route in the other direction, from Bukit Lawang to Berastagi (see page 33). Many of the guides have little experience so check credentials carefully.

Tour operators
The best are those attached to the Sibayak and Ginsata *losmen*. They can arrange canoe or raft trips along the Alas River to the northwest of Berastagi. The journey passes through the Gunung Leuser National Park with traditional villages and tropical rainforest. An all-inclusive 3-day trip, costs US$110. 3-day guided jungle treks are also available for about US$110. Other places worth visiting for tour information include: **CV Berastagi View**, Jln Veteran 4 (inside post office), T0628 92929, brastagiview@yahoo.co.id.
Dinas Parawisata, Tourist Information Service, Jln Gundaling 1, T0628 91084.

⊖ Transport

Berastagi *p36, map p37*
Bus
In order to get to **Parapat** (for Danau Toba) by public bus, it is necessary to change twice: once in Kabanjahe and then in Pemangtangsiantar.

From Berastagi, minibuses and oplets travel to **Kabanjaje** continuously (25 mins, 3000Rp). From there, buses leave for **Pemangtangsiantar** (every 30 mins 0800-1500, 3 hrs, 15000Rp). From Pemangtangsiantar, there are buses to Parapat (every 30 mins, 1 hr, 15,000Rp). There are a couple of alternative and less used routes to **Toba** and **Samosir**. One is to catch a bus to **Haranggaol**, on the north side of Danau Toba. For **Bukit Lawang** catch a Pinang Baris bound bus (2 hrs, 8000Rp), and connect with a Bukit Lawang-bound bus (3 hrs, 15,000Rp).

Tongging
Boat
A boat goes from Tongging to **Haranggaol** every Mon at 0730, which links with the 1500 boat from Haranggaol to **Ambarita**.

Bus
From Berastagi there are direct bus connections with **Tongging**, about 1 per hr in the afternoon, from Jln Kapiten Mumah Purba (10,000Rp). Alternatively, take a bus or bemo to **Kabanjahe** (3000Rp) and from there a minibus to **Simpang Situnggaling** (1 hr, 6000Rp). From here there are minibuses to **Tongging** (1 hr, 6000Rp). Leave enough time as buses only run until about 1600 and there is a lot of hanging around.

❶ Directory

Berastagi *p36, map p37*
Banks There are several banks and money changers in town, and they will change most TCs. Bank Negara Indonesia, Jln Veteran 53. Putra Nusa Mandago Money Changer, Jln Veteran 47. PT Pura Buana International, Jln Veteran. There are 2 authorized Lake Toba money changers, of which Lagundri Tours, Jln Veteran 55, gives the slightly better rate. **Medical services** Health centre, Jln Veteran 30. **Post office** Jln Veteran (by the monument at the top of the road). **Telephone** Wartel office for international telephone calls, Jln Veteran (by the Bank Negara Indonesia).

Danau Toba

Danau Toba and the surrounding countryside is one of the most beautiful areas in Southeast Asia. The cool climate, pine-clothed mountain slopes, the lake and the sprinkling of church spires give the area an almost alpine flavour. After Medan or Padang, it is a welcome relief from the bustle, heat and humidity of the lowlands. The vast inland lake lies 160 km south of Medan and forms the core of Batakland in both a legendary and a geographical sense. The lake covers a total of 1707 sq km and is the largest inland body of water in Southeast Asia (87 km long and 31 km across at its widest point). Lodged in the centre of the lake is Samosir Island, one of Sumatra's most popular destinations (see page 48).

Danau Toba was formed after a massive volcanic explosion 75,000 years ago, not dissimilar – although far more violent – to the one that vaporized Krakatoa in the late 19th century. The eruption of Toba is thought to have been the most powerful eruption in the last million years. The area is now volcanically dormant, the only indication of latent activity being the hot springs on the hill overlooking Pangururan (see page 52). The fact that Danau Toba's water is so warm for a lake at close to 1000 m leads one to assume that there must be some heat underwater too.

Arriving in Danau Toba

Getting there

There is only one way to get to Danau Toba and that is by road. It is 147 km from Berastagi, 176 km from Medan and 509 km from Bukittinggi. The vast majority of visitors either approach from Medan (although some take the troublesome route from Berastagi) or from the south via Padangsidempuan (the road to Bukittinggi and Padang). Taking the Trans-Sumatran Highway from Medan via Tebingtinggi is a fairly fast and direct route, taking about four hours on a good day. The main bus terminal is on Jalan Sisingamangaraja (Jalan SM Raja) – aka the Trans-Sumatran Highway – around 1 km from the centre of town. Some buses stop at bus agencies and others run from the ferry terminal to/from Samosir.

Getting around

Bemos can be hired for 2500Rp for trips around town. There are also various forms of water transport. Danau Toba's two main destinations are the town of Parapat on the mainland and the island of Samosir (see page 48). Buses drop passengers off in Parapat and from here there are regular passenger ferries to Samosir Island. A car ferry runs from Ajibata, just south of Parapat. »» See Transport, pages 46 and 56.

Parapat → For listings, see pages 45-47.

Parapat is a small resort on the east shores of Danau Toba frequented by the Medan wealthy. It was established by the Dutch in the 1930s, although today most Western

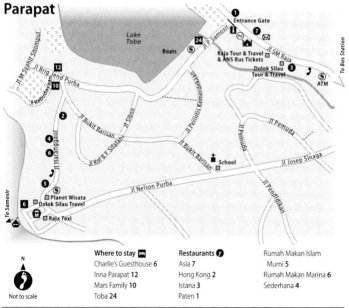

Parapat

N
Not to scale

Where to stay	Restaurants	
Charlie's Guesthouse 6	Asia 7	Rumah Makan Islam
Inna Parapat 12	Hong Kong 2	Murni 5
Mars Family 10	Istana 3	Rumah Makan Marina 6
Toba 24	Paten 1	Sederhana 4

visitors merely breeze through en route to Samosir Island (but must pay 1000Rp entrance for the privilege, although this is not strictly enforced). There are stunning views over the lake, but unfortunately there doesn't seem to have been any coherent attempt to plan the development of the town. This means that there are architectural monstrosities side-by-side with elegant villas.

Parapat has the air of a 1950s European beach resort, with its pedaloes, metal railings, light blue paint and low-rise villa accommodation. This would be a great selling point for nostalgists, but unfortunately all the most attractive hotels are being allowed to slide into ruin, unloved and under-invested. Instead money is being poured into new, large and rather insensitive places. Nowadays, most foreign visitors get out of Parapat as soon as possible and head to the more sedate and rural charms of Samosir.

Tourist information
The tourist office, **Pusat Informasi**, is on Jalan P Samosir, under the archway that welcomes visitors to the town. However, there is virtually no information available here and it is hard to know why it exists.

Places in Parapat
There are few sights in Parapat. The best **beaches** are a little way out of town – like those at Ajibata village, about 1 km south of Parapat – but easily walkable. Saturday is market day when Bataks selling local handicrafts and 'antiques' converge on the town and particularly on the market area at **Pekan Tigaraja**, close to the ferry dock for Samosir. A smaller market is also held here on Tuesday and Thursday. The bright, rust-red roofed church above the town sits in well-cared for gardens, with views over the lake. On Sunday, services have as many as eight to 10 hymns.

Haranggaol → *For listings, see pages 45-47.*

This is a small, sleepy, rather run-down town on Danau Toba's northeastern shore. Few tourists visit the town, but there is an excellent **market** on Monday and Thursday – when there are early morning boat connections with Samosir from Ambarita and/or Simanindo – and good walks in the surrounding countryside. If visitors wish to experience the wonder of Toba, without the crowds at Parapat and on Samosir, then this is the place to come.

Arriving in Haranggaol
Haranggaol lies off the main bus route, so it can take a time to reach the town. There are bus connections from Kabanjahe (easily accessible from Berastagi) to Seribudolok, and from there bemos run to Haranggaol. Getting to or from Parapat to Haranggaol is not easy; it involves three bus changes and it usually takes eight hours to cover the 50-odd km. Taking the ferry is easier. ➡ *See Transport, page 47.*

Danau Toba listings

For hotel and restaurant price codes and other relevant information, see pages 8-10.

⊖ Where to stay

Parapat *p43, map p43*
Most tourists merely breeze though Parapat on market day or on their way to or from Samosir. However, there is a fair range of options for those who miss the last ferry or have an early morning bus to catch.
$$$-$$ Hotel Inna Parapat, Jln Marihat 1, T0625 41012. With a distinct 1970s design, this 3-star hotel has a range of comfortable rooms with TV and bath. The rooms at the back are best, with beautiful views of the lake, and a balcony. There is a good swimming beach and jet skis for hire. Free Wi-Fi access in the lobby. Discounts available (30%).
$$ Toba Hotel, Jln Pulo Samosir 8, T0625 41073. Though the corridors here are virtually pitch black at noon and the furniture is rather ancient, the rooms are right on the shoreline, and there is access to a beach and relaxed outdoors seating. Upstairs rooms are comfortable, with better views.
$$-$ Mars Family Hotel, Jln Kebudayaan 1, T0625 41459. The cheap rooms here are dark, but clean. Paying a little more gets a spotless room, with lake views and TV. Peaceful and well-run hotel. Recommended.
$ Charlie's Guesthouse, Tigaraja, T0625 41277. The owner of this place is a popular Batak pop star, and speaks English with the peculiar cockney accent the locals develop here. Near the harbour for boats to Tuk Tuk, so is ideal for late-night arrivals intending on leaving town the next morning. Homely and chaotic hotel with simple and comfortable rooms, although a little dark.

Haranggaol *p44*
$ Haranggaol, situated in town rather than on the lake shore. The best place to stay. Some rooms have hot water. There's a large eating area, used to catering for tour groups.

$ Segumba Cottages, 3 km out of town. Bali-style cottages situated in a beautiful, quiet position. Some rooms with *mandi*.

🍴 Restaurants

Parapat *p43, map p43*
There are 2 concentrations of restaurants: on **Jln Haranggaol** and along **Jln Sisingamangaraja**. Haranggaol restaurants are geared more to tourists, while locals and Indonesians tend to eat at those on Jln Sisingamangaraja. The Indonesian (and Chinese) restaurants along Jln Sisingamangaraja are generally better than those on Jln Haranggaol.
$ Hong Kong, Jln Harangaol 91, T0625 41395. Daily 0800-2100. Clean place serving up good portions of Chinese food and a smattering of Western fare. Recommended.
$ Istana, Jln SM Raja 68, towards the bus terminal. Good *nasi Padang*. Recommended.
$ Paten, Jln SM Raja (opposite the entrance gateway to Parapat). One of the better Chinese restaurants in this strip. Well priced.
$ Restoran Asia, Jln SM Raja 80-82, T0625 41450. Daily 0700-2200. Chinese and Indonesian food, with excellent seafood and sweet-and-sour dishes. Also some fair steaks.
$ Rumah Makan Islam Murni, Jln Harangaol 84. Daily 0700-2200. Small but tasty selection of Malay cuisine. The *nasi soto* (chicken in rich coconut-based soup with potato patty served with rice) is excellent.
$ Rumah Makan Marina, Jln Harangaol 48. Daily 0800-2100. Indonesian dishes, clean.
$ Sederhana, Jln Haranggaol 38. One of the best Padang restaurants in town, good *kangkung*, clean and well-run.

🎭 Entertainment

Parapat *p43, map p43*
Batak cultural shows are held on public holidays and during the **Danau Toba Festival** in Jun at the Open Air Stage

on Jln Kebudayaan. The more expensive hotels (eg Inna Parapat) also sometimes organize cultural shows.

✿ Festivals

Parapat *p43, map p43*
Jun/Jul Pesta Danau Toba (Danau Toba Festival) (movable), held over a week. Hardly traditional, but there are various cultural performances and canoe races on the lake.

◎ Shopping

Parapat *p43, map p43*
Jln Sisingamangaraja and Jln Haranggaol are the main shopping areas, and both have the same type of souvenir shops. **Batak Culture Art Shop**, towards the bottom of Jln Haranggaol, is better than most and sells some authentic Batak pieces. There's a market at **Pekan Tigaraja** near the ferry jetty, on Sat – a good place to buy batik and handicrafts. On other mornings there is a small food market.

◉ What to do

Parapat *p43, map p43*
Cruises
Boats can be hired from near the **Toba Hotel**. Trips around Samosir cost US$137, or a 1-hr ride around the lake can be had for US$44. These prices are highly ambitious and good bargaining should bring the price down significantly.

Rafting
Day-trips down the Asahan River (80 km from Parapat) for US$80 per person (minimum 2 people). Price includes all equipment, food and transportation.

Swimming
There is a decent beach for swimming in front of the **Hotel Inna Parapat**.

Tour operators
Tour companies in Parapat have gained a rather poor reputation. Usually they are just used to book bus tickets and confirm flights, rather than arrange tours.
Dolok Silau, Jln S Raja 56 and at the harbour near **Charlie's Guesthouse**, T0625 41467. ANS bus tickets to destinations in Sumatra and beyond. Also arranges rafting trips down the Asahan River.
Planet Wisata, Jln Haranggaol 97, T0625 41037. Bus and plane tickets. Also books AirAsia flights.
Raja Taxi, Tigaraja, opposite **Charlie's Guesthouse**. Minibuses to Medan.

Watersports
Water-scooters and pedal boats on the waterfront and from the **Hotel Inna Parapat**.

⊖ Transport

Parapat *p43, map p43*
Boat
Parapat is the main port for **Samosir Island**, and ferries leave the town from the jetty in the Tigaraja market at the bottom of Jln Haranggaol (0930-1730, 30 mins, 7000Rp). Most ferries dock at Tuk Tuk on Samosir and they will drop off at the various hotel jetties, so state your destination. Some continue north to Ambarita, while others also dock at Tomok just south of the Tuk Tuk Peninsula. Most of the hotels and guesthouses have a ferry timetable posted. For further details, see page 56. Note that arriving after dark makes it difficult to reach Samosir the same day. The only ferry operating after 1930 is the car ferry (see below). For those who arrive in Parapat after the last ferry has departed, and can't bear the thought of spending a night in town, it is possible to charter a boat for around US$40 (bargain hard).
Car ferry There is a car ferry from Ajibata, just south of town, to **Tomok**, every 3 hrs, 0830-2130, 4000Rp for foot passengers, 150,000Rp for a car.

Bus

There are no direct buses to **Berastagi** –
it is necessary first to travel to
Pemangtangsiantar (1 hr, 15,000Rp), and
then change to a **Kebonjahe** bus (3 hrs,
15,000Rp), before finally getting on a bus
bound for **Berastagi** (25 mins, 3000Rp).

For **Medan**, minibuses pick passengers
up off the ferry from Tuk Tuk and drive to
the Amplas terminal (5 hrs, 60,000Rp). More
comfortable minibuses are available from
Raja Taxi (see Tour operators) for 80,000Rp.

Economy buses to Medan depart
from the terminal on Jln SM Raja (6 hrs,
25,000Rp), and drop passengers at Medan's
Amplas terminal. Other destinations include
Bukittingi (15 hrs, economy US$12, a/c
executive US$19); **Padang** (17 hrs, economy
US$15, a/c executive US$22); **Jakarta**
(50 hrs, economy US$40, a/c executive
US$60). For masochists there are buses to
Yogyakarta and **Denpasar**, which are more
expensive than flights and take days.

Note It is much more expensive getting
tickets from travel agencies and hotels in
Parapat and Tuk Tuk, than buying them
directly from the bus station. Prices given
above reflect prices of tickets bought at
the bus station. **Andilo Nancy**, Parapat bus
terminal, T0625 41548, sells ANS tickets
for a/c buses to **Bukittinggi**. Avoid seats
numbered 33, 34 and 35 as these are right
at the back of the bus next to the toilet and
do not recline.

Haranggaol *p44*
Boat

A ferry connects Haranggaol with **Tuk
Tuk** and **Ambarita** on Samosir Island
on Mon and Thu at 1300 and 1500, 4 hrs.
See page 56 for the time of journeys in
the other direction. From Samosir there
are many ferries across to **Parapat** for
onward buses to Berastagi and Medan.

🛈 Directory

Parapat *p43, map p43*
Banks Rates are poor in Parapat, but
even worse on Samosir. It is best to
arrive with sufficient cash for your stay,
although that may present risks in itself.
There is a series of places that will change
money on Jln Haranggaol and in the
market area. **Bank Rakyat Indonesia**, Jln
Sisingamangaraja (almost opposite the
bus terminal). **Pura Buana International**,
Jln Haranggaol 75, money changer.
Medical services Hospital, Jln P Samosir.
Police Jln Sisingamangaraja (close to
the inter-section with Jln P Samosir).
Post office Jln Sisingamangaraja 90.
Telephone Warpostel, Jln Haranggaol
74 (for fax and telephone), the most
conveniently located of the telephone
offices; **Warpostel** at Jln Sisingamangarja
72 (for fax and international telephone).

Samosir Island

With a large number of traditional Batak villages, fine examples of *rumah adat* (traditional houses), cemeteries, churches, enigmatic stone carvings, good swimming, hiking, cheap lodgings and few cars, Samosir Island has proved a favourite destination for travellers. Surrounded by the lake and mist-cloaked mountains, which rise precipitously from the narrow 'coastal' strip on the eastern shore, it is one of the most naturally beautiful and romantic spots in Southeast Asia.

Accommodation is concentrated on the Tuk Tuk Peninsula, Tomok and Ambarita, although there are basic guesthouses scattered across the island. Rooms with a lake view are double the price of those without. Camping is also easy on Samosir. Food on the island is good and cheap; there are a number of *warungs* in Tomok, Ambarita and on the Tuk Tuk Peninsula.

Arriving on Samosir Island → *Phone code: 0645.*

Getting there
There are regular passenger ferries to Samosir Island from Danau Toba. It is possible to charter a speedboat for around US$40 (bargain hard). A car ferry runs from Ajibata, just south of Parapat. Passenger ferries drop passengers off at various points on the Tuk Tuk Peninsula, usually close to their chosen guesthouse or hotel. The crossing takes about 35 minutes. ▶ *See Transport, pages 46 and 56.*

Getting around
Numerous guesthouses and tour companies have motorbikes for hire, in varying states of repair. Prices vary accordingly but range between US$6-8 per day. A driving licence is not required. This is a recommended way to see the island, although accidents are all too frequent on the narrow roads. Note that although it is possible to drive across the island, there is no assistance available should you get a puncture – which means a long walk to the nearest motorbike repair outfit. Better still, hire a bicycle and slow the pace or embark on a hike or a walk.

A minibus runs every 20 minutes in the morning between Tomok and Ambarita, and then on to Pangururan; less frequently in the afternoons. The bus does not take the route around the lakeshore on the Tuk Tuk Peninsula – it cuts across the neck of the peninsula.

Places on Samosir Island → For listings, see pages 53-57.

The various places of interest on Samosir are listed under the town entries below. However, there are two aspects of the island that are everywhere. First there are the **tombs**. These can be seen throughout the Batak area, but it is on Samosir where people find themselves, so to speak, face to face with them. Some are comparatively modest affairs: the tomb itself is topped with a restrained Batak house made of brick and stucco. Others are grandiose structures, with several storeys, pillars and ostentatious ornamentation. Still others seem to be tongue-in-cheek: the one surmounted with a Christmas tree, decorated with fairy lights just out of Ambarita on the road to Simanindo, is a case in point. All, though, show an imaginative fusion of Batak tradition and Christian symbolism. The need to construct these tombs must have been strong (the tradition is dying) as many took up valuable rice land.

The other aspect of Samosir are the **fish 'tanks'** known as *deke ramba*. These have been laboriously constructed on the lake edge, rocks carefully fashioned and then placed close enough together to allow the water in, while also keeping the fish in. Some appear to be very old, and most are still in use. Many have become ornamental, containing sometimes gargantuan *ikan mas*; others are still used to raise fish for the pot. The main fish raised are *ikan mas* (which are also eaten) and *mujahir*, which are native to Danau Toba. Fingerlings are caught in the lake and then raised in the tanks for about two years before being sold.

Tomok
Situated around 3 km south of the Tuk Tuk Peninsula, this was a traditional Batak village. and is a popular day-trip from Parapat. This means that there are a host of souvenir stalls, drinks shops and *warungs*, but none that you would go out of your way to patronize. Tomok is also the docking point for the car ferry, which means that lorries roar through this rather sad place.

However, the town is not an entirely lost cause, as it contains some fine high-prowed **Batak houses** and **carved stone coffins, elephants** and **chairs**. Walking from the jetty inland, there is a path lined with souvenir stalls that winds up a small hill. Half way up (about 500 m) is the **Museum of King Soribunto Sidabutar** ① *admission by donation (about 2000Rp)*, housed in a traditional Batak house, containing a small number of Batak implements and photographs of the family.

Walking a little further up the hill, on from the mass of stalls and taking the path to the right, there is a carved stone coffin, the **King's Coffin**, protected by what remains of a large but dying *hariam* tree. The sarcophagus contains the body of Raja Sidabutar, the chief of the first tribe to migrate to the area. The coffin is surrounded by stone elephants, figures, tables and chairs. Further up the main path, past the stalls, is another grave site with stone figures arranged in a circle. The **church services** at the town and elsewhere on Samosir are worthwhile for the enthusiasm of the congregations – choose between no fewer than three churches.

Tuk Tuk Peninsula
Tuk Tuk is the name given to the peninsula that juts out rather inelegantly from the main body of Samosir Island, about 4 km north of Tomok. It is really just a haven for tourists, with nothing of cultural interest. There is a continuous ribbon of hotels, guesthouses, restaurants, minimarts, curio shops and tour companies following the road that skirts the perimeter of the peninsula. This might sound pretty dire, but in fact the development is not as overbearing as it might be – the nature of the topography means that you don't get confronted with a vision of tourism hell. And in spite of the rapid development, Tuk Tuk is still a peaceful spot, with

good swimming, sometimes great food and good-value accommodation. There are various places on Tuk Tuk that masquerade as **tourist information centres**, when they are actually tour companies and travel agents. Nonetheless, they can be a good source of information.

If you decide to walk, it will take approximately one hour to get to Tomok and 1½ hours to reach Ambarita. Mountain bikes can be hired from many of the guesthouses and hotels for 25,000Rp per day and this is a recommended way to see the island; make sure you check over the bike carefully. Motorbikes can be hired for US$6-8 per day.

1 Tuk Tuk Peninsula

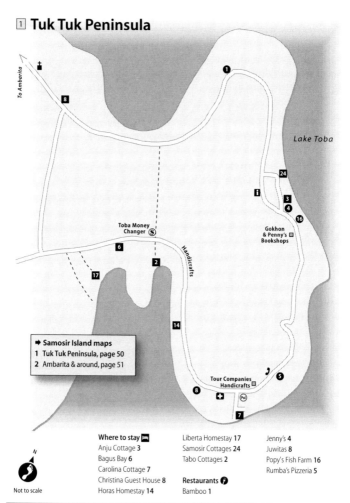

Where to stay 🛏
Anju Cottage 3
Bagus Bay 6
Carolina Cottage 7
Christina Guest House 8
Horas Homestay 14

Liberta Homestay 17
Samosir Cottages 24
Tabo Cottages 2

Restaurants 🍴
Bamboo 1

Jenny's 4
Juwitas 8
Popy's Fish Farm 16
Rumba's Pizzeria 5

N
Not to scale

Ambarita

The pretty town of Ambarita, on the lakeshore north of Tuk Tuk, has more in the way of sights but nowhere to stay. There are guesthouses and hotels along the road running north towards Simanindo and the track that follows the coast to Tuk Tuk. Most visitors staying in these hotels rent their own wheels from Tuk Tuk. If you choose to walk allow 1½ hours to Tuk Tuk; seven hours to reach Simanindo at the north tip of the island.

Places in Ambarita There are several **megalithic complexes** in the vicinity of the town. The most important of which is near the jetty at **Siallagan village** ⓘ *2000Rp*. There are lots of 'freelance' guides waiting to pounce on tourists here, some of whom explain the sight quite dramatically. Expect to pay between US$1-3 for a tour. The first group of chairs, arranged under a hariam tree, are 300 years old and were used as the site for village councils, where disputes were settled and punishments decided. The chief would sit in the armchair, while other village elders sat in the surrounding chairs. The person on trial would sit on the small chair closest to the table – having been incarcerated for seven days in the small cage close to the stone chairs. A medicine man would consult his diary to decide on the best day for any sentence to be meted out. A stone figure mysteriously occupies one of the seats. Guides hang around to recount the chairs' gruesome past with a certain amount of relish. The really gruesome part of the traditional legal system is associated with the second group of megaliths. The criminal sentenced to death would be blindfolded, tied hand and foot and carried to the large stone block. He would then be sliced with a small knife and chilli, garlic and onions were reputedly rubbed into the wounds before a mallet – like a meat tenderizer – would be used to prepare the 'meat' for consumption (by pounding the man, already, no doubt, in a certain amount of pain). Having been sufficiently trussed and pummelled, the unfortunate would be carried to the block and his head cut off. The (strength-giving) blood was collected and drunk by the chief, while the meat was distributed to the villagers.

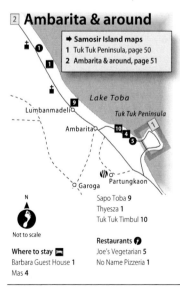

Lake Toba
Lumbanmadeli
Tuk Tuk Peninsula
Ambarita
Garoga   Partungkaon

N
Not to scale

Sapo Toba **9**
Thyesza **1**
Tuk Tuk Timbul **10**

Restaurants ⓕ
Joe's Vegetarian **5**
No Name Pizzeria **1**

Where to stay 🛏
Barbara Guest House **1**
Mas **4**

The bones, finally, were collected up and thrown into the lake – which was unclean for a week and no activity occurred during this time. The chief's staff is carved with the faces of past chiefly generations. This gruesome tradition came to an end in 1816 when a German missionary (by the name of Nommensen – there's a university in Medan named after him) converted the population to Christianity. Facing the complex is a row of well-preserved **Batak houses**.

Also here is the **tomb of Laga Siallagan**, the first chief of Ambarita. To get there, turn right (coming from Tomok) off the main road in Ambarita, shortly after the post office walk past the football field and police post, and turn left to walk past tombs and ricefields to the complex, about 500 m in all, it is possible to approach from Tuk Tuk via the side road.

Simanindo

Simanindo is at the north tip of Samosir. The house of a former Batak chief, Raja Simalungun, has been restored and turned into an **Ethnological Museum** (**Huta Bolon**) ① *daily 1000-1700, 5000Rp,* containing a musty collection of Batak, Dutch and Chinese artefacts. The brief labels in English reveal little. There are souvenirs for sale in Batak houses.

Close by is a well-preserved fortified **Batak community** ① *shows are staged Mon-Sat 1030-1110, 1145-1239, and Sun 1145-1230, if a minimum of 5 tourists show up, 30,000Rp,* with fine examples of richly carved Batak houses. This is the best maintained of the various 'preserved' communities on Samosir. Visitors sit through a lengthy sequence of 12 dances, performed by a rather lacklustre crew – many of the dances seem more like loosening up exercises prior to a workout. The requisite audience participation number and the final dance gives an opportunity for guests to add a donation to their entrance fee.

Pangururan

Pangururan, the capital of Samosir, is on the west coast, close to the point where the island is attached to the mainland by a small bridge. It is a dusty, ramshackle little town. There is no reason to stay here and most people visit the town on the way to the **hot springs** on Mount Belirang. Pangururan is also probably the best place from which to set out to hike across the island to Tomok (see Hiking, page 56).

From Pangururan, a bus service operates to the interior village of Roonggurni Huta. An occasional service has begun operating in the south part of the island between Tomok and Nainggolan, and then on to Pangururan.

Mount Belirang hot springs

① *2.5 km or 1 hr from Pangururan if you walk, 1000Rp.*

The sulphurous gases and water have killed the vegetation on the hillside, leaving a white residue – the scar can be seen from a long way off on Samosir. Cross the stone bridge and turn right (north). They are about a third of the way up Mount Belirang (also known as Mount Pusuk Buhit). It is too hot to bathe at the point where they emerge from the ground, but lower down there are pools where visitors can soak in the healing sulphurous waters. There are separate bathing pools for men and women and some *warungs* nearby for refreshments. Views of the lake are spoilt by uncontrolled, unattractive development, and even the spring site itself leaves rather a lot to be desired: plastic pipes and moulded concrete make it look, in places, more like a plumber's training site.

Samosir Island listings

For hotel and restaurant price codes and other relevant information, see pages 8-10.

⊙ Where to stay

Tuk Tuk Peninsula *p49, map p50*
Tuk Tuk is almost overloaded with lodgings, from very simple affairs to large, comfortable hotels. Almost all accommodation is situated along the road (really just a lane) that skirts around the edge of the peninsula. To the north and south there is a relatively steep drop into the lake, so the chalets seem to cling precariously to the hillside. To the east the land slopes more gently into the lake, so there is room for larger gardens and bigger guesthouses and hotels. Be sure to bargain for your accommodation; stays of 3 or more nights often see prices dropping sharply.
$$$-$ Tabo Cottages, T0625 451318, www.tabocottages.com. Those in the know stay here, in beautiful Batak cottages overlooking a large garden and the lake. The mid-priced rooms are clean and have hot water, and some have outdoor bathrooms. Economy rooms are good value, with cold water and lake views. There's also a smashing vegetarian restaurant. Recommended.
$$-$ Samosir Cottages, T0625 41050, www.samosircottages.com. Sprawling and impersonal resort-style place that fills up with Indonesian tourists at weekends. Rooms are clean and the family room can sleep 4 and has cable TV, fridge and kitchen. Internet access available (expensive).
$ Anju Cottage, T0625 451265. Good selection of rooms, ranging from Batak houses to tiled concrete chalets in a breezy setting. There is decent swimming here and a diving board. Prices include breakfast.
$ Bagus Bay, T0625 451287. Well-run and friendly place with a selection of spotless rooms in Batak houses, some with lake views. 4 attractive rooms set in a leafy

garden. Extensive gardens with badminton and volleyball courts and children's play area. Good range of facilities including Internet café, 10,000Rp per hr, book exchange and satellite TV in the restaurant. Recommended.
$ Carolina Cottage, T0625 41520, carolina@indosat.net.id. By far the most popular place in Toba, with convenient access from Parapat, excellent swimming area with pontoon for diving, and well-manicured gardens. Selection of rooms in Batak houses, most with great lake views, the more expensive rooms have hot water and a breezy balcony. Recommended.
$ Christina Guest House, T0625 451027. On the road heading out towards Ambarita, rooms here are comfortable and fronted by an attractive lily pond with expansive views of the lake. The family house is superb value, with space for 5 people. There is a restaurant with cable TV. Internet café.
$ Horas Homestay, T081 3960 13643. Access to these rooms is via **Horas Chillout Café**, and down crumbling and overgrown steps that lead to the shoreline. Basic clean rooms. This place possesses a rural charm not found in most other Tuk Tuk lodgings and will satisfy those in need of some peace and quiet.
$ Liberta Homestay, T0625 451035. Collection of Batak houses, some in a better state of repair than others, set in a lovely garden. This is a popular place, and gets busy at weekends. Locals bring along their guitars for musical evenings, and often like to challenge visitors to games of chess in the laid-back restaurant. Recommended.
$ Sibigo, down a small track next to **Carolina**, T0625 451017. Sleepy and quiet. Rooms are adequate and have beautiful views, but are sorely in need of a good clean.

Ambarita *p51, map p51*
The hotels and guesthouses listed here are scattered along the road towards

Simanindo (over a distance of about 9 km from town) and the smaller road leading towards Tuk Tuk (over about 2 km). They are quieter than those in Tuk Tuk. They are also quite isolated, so you will need to hire a bicycle or motorcyle if you want to try other restaurants and bars. This part of the island is also rather treeless near the lake shore, but has some good swimming. Guesthouse owners will often pick visitors up from Tomok or Tuk Tuk if they phone ahead. Otherwise, catch a minibus from Tomok heading towards Simanindo (3000Rp) and tell the driver which hotel you wish to alight at. All the hotels mentioned have restaurant attached.

$$ Sapo Toba, T0625 700009. Collection of smart chalets built on a hillside overlooking the lake. All the rooms are identical and have hot water, TV, fridge and bathroom with bath. The reception is at the bottom of the hillside inside the restaurant on the left, just keep following those eternal steps down. Internet 35,000Rp per hr.

$ Barbara Guest House, T0625 41230. Down a small track and neighbouring **Thyesza**, accommodation is a little down at heel, but the friendly staff makes up for peeling paint. Some rooms have a lake view and hot water. Restaurant and good swimming.

$ Mas, T0625 451051. Gorgeous views, a peaceful setting and a good selection of clean tiled rooms in a concrete block fronted by a small fish farm with swirling koi. This is a fine option for those wishing to stay far enough outside of Tuk Tuk to escape the overtly touristy atmosphere, but close enough to have good dining options nearby. Tuk Tuk is a leisurely 30-min stroll away. Rooms downstairs have hot water. Recommended.

$ Thyesza, 4 km to the north of Ambarita, down a small track leading to the shoreline, T0625 41443, www.flowerofsamosir.com. Well-maintained place with 6 tidy tiled rooms in a flower covered concrete block slightly set back from the lake. Also a

cheaper Batak house right on the shore. This part of the coast has excellent swimming and clear water. The restaurant is good. Recommended.

$ Tuk Tuk Timbul, about 1 km south of Ambarita towards Tuk Tuk, T0625 41374. Collection of smart cottages in a great isolated position off the road and down on the lakefront on a small headland. The restaurant serves good food including home-baked bread. There is a large fish pond and good swimming.

❷ Restaurants

Tomok p49
There are several *warung* around the village, eg **Islam**. Nothing outstanding, but passable whether European, Chinese, Minang or standard Indonesian fare.

Tuk Tuk Peninsula p49, map p50
There is an increasing number of good restaurants on Tuk Tuk; many specialize in vegetarian travellers' food.

$ Bamboo. Daily 0800-2200. Good spot for sunsets, cocktails and a range of simple Western food and Indonesian staples. The best option here is the beach BBQ when the owner grills fresh lake fish and serves them with a variety of lip-smacking sauces.

$ Jenny's. Daily 0800-2200. Popular place with friendly staff in a colourful setting serving sandwiches and good salads. There is often live Batak folk music here in the evenings.

$ Juwitas, T0625 451217. Daily 0800-2200. Small wooden café with chatty owner serving decent vegetarian grub, curries and lake fish.

$ Popy's Fish Farm, T0625 451291. Daily 0800-2200. Fresh fish cooked in every conceivable way in a breezy setting. The menu also features some Chinese dishes and curries.

$ Rumba's Pizzeria, there are 2 branches. One is on the southeastern side of the peninsula, T0625 451310, daily 0800-2300, reasonable create-your-own pizza with a variety of toppings. The other is on the western side of the peninsula, T0625 451045, daily 1200-2100, considerably cheaper, with sunset views and good pizzas. Recommended.

Guesthouse restaurants
Some of the best dining is in Tuk Tuk's guesthouses, which generally serve food daily 0700-2200.

$ Bagus Bay. Pizza, tasty veg curry and a breakfast menu featuring rare treats such as baked beans with cheese on toast.

$ Liberta Homestay. Mellow setting for a beer, healthy grub with lots of vegetarian offerings in a convivial setting.

$ Sibigo. Excellent fresh lake fish grilled and served with limes and local sauces. This place also serves chips with all manner of sauces including *sate* and *sambal*.

$ Tabo Cottages. This is a haven for vegetarians with hearty soups accompanied by fresh bread, good salads and aloe vera power drinks. Carnivores are not forgotten, with a few fish and chicken dishes on the menu. There is a good breakfast menu here, with a superb-value buffet breakfast. At weekends the kitchen struggles to cope with demand and it can take some time for meals to materialize. Recommended.

Ambarita *p51, map p51*
There are a couple of coffee shops and *warungs* in town, but nothing that stands out. The best place to eat is at a nice little *warung* next to the police post (turn off the main road and walk past the football field).

$ Joe's Vegetarian Restaurant, Pindu Raya (a hamlet between Tuk Tuk and Ambarita). Known for its home-made cakes and coffee.

$ No Name Pizzeria, 7 km or so north of town on the road to Simanindo just in front of the **King's Hotel**. Curiously, there is currently no pizza on offer despite the name, but the menu features simple Western food and some standard

Indonesian dishes. This place doubles up as a *tuak* (toddy) shop at night and can be a fun place to meet locals.

Guesthouse restaurants
Of the guesthouses on the strip between Ambarita and Simanindo, **Barbara's** and **Thyesza** (both **$**) are the most traveller savvy, and **Thyesza** cooks up authentic Batak dishes (including dog meat on request), simple Western fare and serves excellent fresh fruit juices including refreshing *marquisa* juice.

Bars and clubs

Tuk Tuk Peninsula *p49, map p50*
Locals head to *tuak* (toddy) shops of an evening for a drink and chat. These can look fairly inconspicuous from the outside. Ask at your hotel which one is most accessible. Expect to pay 1500 to 2000Rp for a glass.
Brando's Blues Bar, T0625 451084. Open 1800-0200. Reggae, blues and a smattering of house music at this place, which has a small dance floor, some outdoors seating, a pool table and cheap, strong spirits to get the legs swaying to a different tune.

Entertainment

Tuk Tuk Peninsula *p49, map p50*
Traditional dance Batak folk song and dance performances every Wed and Sat, 2015 at **Bagus Bay** (see Where to stay). A very popular and a fun way to spend an evening.

Shopping

Tuk Tuk Peninsula *p49, map p50*
Books Gokhon Bookshop, offers a postal service; **Bagus Bay Bookshop**, for second-hand novels; **Penny's Bookshop**, has an excellent book-lending section, maps and some DVDs to rent – for 8000Rp you can watch a DVD in the shop. There are a number of other places around the

peninsula that sell second-hand books.
Crafts There are scores of craft and curio shops selling woodcarvings, medicine books, leather goods, Batak calendars, carved chess sets and wind chimes. The chess sets are a good buy here but they vary enormously in quality and price, it's worth shopping around.

⊙ What to do

Samosir Island *p48*
Hiking
Hiking across Samosir's central highlands is one of the most rewarding ways to see the island. The distance from east to west is only about 20 km as the crow flies, but the route is a steep and circuitous climb of 750 m, making the real walking distance about 45 km. It is just possible to walk the route in a day if hiking from west to east (eg from Pangururan to Tomok), but it is best to stay overnight at the interior village of Roonggurni Huta to recuperate from the climb. A number of homestays here charge about US$2-3 for a bed.

The hike from Roonggurni Huta to Tomok or vice versa is about 29 km: 10 hrs if walking uphill, 6 hrs down. There are also trails to Ambarita and (longer still) to Tuk Tuk, although these are less well marked. From Roonggurni Huta to Pangururan it is a less steep 17 km, about 3 hrs walking. There is also a bus service for the terminally exhausted between Pangururan and Roonggurni Huta. It is probably best to climb from west to east as this misses out the steep climb up to Roonggurni Huta from Tomok. Catch a bus to Pangururan and set off from there. A map marking the hiking trails and giving more details about the routes is available from **Penny's Bookshop** in Tuk Tuk.

Tours
There are no regular tours around the island, due to lack of tourists, but they can be arranged at one of the tour companies. Most of the hotels will provide a map, and suggest a coherent day-trip itinerary taking in Tomok, Siallangan, Sangkal (weaving village), Simanindo, and over to the hot springs near Pangguran. Many of the guys working in the hotels will offer to guide tourists for US$5-10.

Tuk Tuk Peninsula *p49, map p50*
Cooking classes
Juwita's (see Restaurants). Visitors can choose from a list of Batak and Indonesian dishes and learn to cook them with the vivacious owner in a 3-hr class, US$20 (negotiable).

Massage
Traditional massage available at guesthouses around the peninsula, about 50,000Rp per session. Ask at **Tabo Cottages** or **Bagus Bay**.

Tour operators
There are plenty of operators around the peninsular, browse for a good price. The companies listed here will book bus tickets (very expensive – cheaper from the **Audilo Nancy** office at the bus terminal) and help arrange a tour of the island:
Anju Cottage, T0625 451265.
Bagus Bay Information, T0625 451287.

⊖ Transport

Samosir Island *p48*
Boat
Most visitors get to Samosir by ferry from **Parapat**. The ferry leaves about every hour and takes 30 mins (7000Rp). Most ferries dock at Tuk Tuk on Samosir and they will drop off at the various hotel jetties, so state your destination. Some continue north to **Ambarita**, while others also dock at **Tomok** just south of the Tuk Tuk Peninsula. Most of the hotels and guesthouses have a ferry timetable posted. Check the schedule.

The 1st ferry from Parapat leaves at 0930, from Samosir at 0730. The last departs Parapat at 1730, Samosir at 1630.

The **car ferry service** from Ajibata, just south of Parapat (see map, page 43) to Tomok, runs every 3 hrs from 0830-1730 with a final sailing at 2130, 4000Rp for foot passengers, 150,000Rp for a car.

A ferry also links Tuk Tuk and Ambarita with **Haranggaol** on Danau Toba's north shore, but this only runs on Mon – market day in Haranggaol. The ferry leaves Ambarita at 0700 and takes 2-3 hrs, largely because it stops to pick up market-goers all along the eastern shore. See Haranggaol Transport, page 47. For onwards buses from Parapat, see page 47.

Tomok *p49*
Bus
In theory, a bus runs every 20 mins to **Pangururan** and all stops along the route.

Car ferry
There is a car ferry to **Ajibata**, just south of Parapat (see map, page 43) every 3 hrs 0830-1730, last departure at 2100, 4000Rp for foot passengers, 150,000Rp for a car.

Tuk Tuk Peninsula *p49, map p50*
Boat
Ferry connections with **Parapat** about every hour, 7000Rp.

Bus
Walk to the main road to catch one of the buses running between **Tomok** and **Pangururan**, every 20 mins, 12,000Rp.

Ambarita *p51, map p51*
Bus
Connections every 20 mins with **Tomok**, 3000Rp, and all stops to **Pangururan**.

⊙ Directory

Samosir Island *p48*
Banks Rates of exchange on Samosir are poor, worse than in Parapat, although the larger hotels and some travel agents will change TCs and cash. There is also a money changer in Ambarita. **Telephone** International calls can be placed from many of the hotels and tour and travel agencies.

Tomok *p49*
Telephone Wartel office, on the northern edge of town on the main road.

Tuk Tuk Peninsula *p49, map p50*
Banks PT Andilo Nancy travel agent changes money at a better rate than other places. **Internet** Tabo Cottages and Bagus Bay. **Medical services** Clinic (Puskesmas), on the southern side of the peninsula. **Post office** No post office but many places sell stamps and will post letters. **Telephone** Many guesthouses, hotels and tour companies offer IDD phone facilities and fax.

Ambarita *p51, map p51*
Banks Bank Rakyat Indonesia on Jln Raya (the main road). **Medical services** Clinic (Puskemas), in town. **Post office** Jln Raya 39, on the right-hand side from Tomok, shortly before the turning for the Siallangan megalithic complex.

Bukittinggi and around

Visitors to West Sumatra spend most of their time based in and around the highland settlement of Bukittinggi, its cultural heart. This is entirely understandable as it is one of the most attractive towns in Sumatra and has many places of interest in the immediate vicinity. The accommodation is good, the climate invigorating and the food excellent. The highly mobile Minang people who view this area as their ancestral home are fascinating, and the surrounding countryside is some of the most beautiful in Sumatra. There are peaceful highland lakes, like Maninjau and Singkarak, rivers for rafting and mountain treks.

In July 2008, Bukittinggi was thrust into the international limelight as Indonesian police foiled a plot by Jemaah Islamiyah to blow up the Bedual Café. The suspects, who were arrested in Palembang, claimed that the bombs had at one stage even been put inside the café. However, they realized that with the downturn of tourism in Sumatra, any attack would in fact take more Muslim lives than tourist lives, and subsequently pulled out.

Arriving in Bukittinggi → *Phone code: 0752.*

Getting there
The nearest airport is on the fringes of Padang, a two-hour bus journey away. Most people get to this popular destination by bus; the journey overland from Medan via Danau Toba is pretty gruelling, just over 500 km or 15 hours' drive in total (if the bus doesn't break down, an all too frequent occurrence), however, owing to its popularity, the range of buses and destinations is impressive for a town that is relatively small. ▶▶ *See Transport, page 69.*

Getting around
Bukittinggi itself is small and cool enough to negotiate on foot. One of the great attractions is the surrounding countryside, but trying to get around on public transport can be a bit of a drag so many visitors choose to charter a bemo, hire a motorbike or bicycle, or take a tour. Bemos cost about 2000Rp per trip. Motorbikes and mountain bikes can be hired from many guesthouses and tour companies; motorbike hire costs about 65,000Rp per day and mountain bikes 25,000Rp.

Visitors arriving at Aur Kuning may be encouraged to take a taxi to town; regular (red) opelet ply the route for a fraction of the price (2000Rp), or a bemo can be chartered for the trip to Jalan A Yani for 15,000Rp.

The geographic and functional centre of Bukittinggi is marked by a strange-looking **clock tower** at the south end of Jalan Jend A Yani, the town's main thoroughfare. The Jam Gadang, or 'Great Clock' as it is known, was built by the Dutch in 1827. It is a veritable Sumatran 'Big Ben' and has a Minangkabau-style roof perched uneasily on the top. The **central market** is close to the clock tower. Although there is a market every day of the week, market day is

Bukittinggi

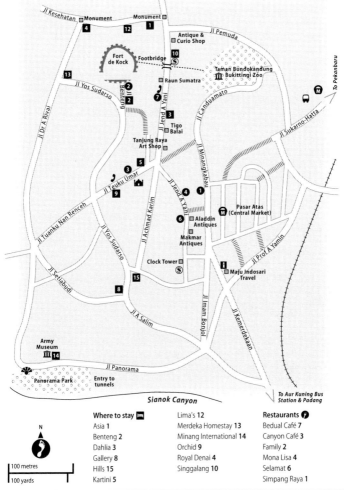

Where to stay 🛏	Lima's **12**	Restaurants 🍴
Asia **1**	Merdeka Homestay **13**	Bedual Café **7**
Benteng **2**	Minang International **14**	Canyon Café **3**
Dahlia **3**	Orchid **9**	Family **2**
Gallery **8**	Royal Denai **4**	Mona Lisa **4**
Hills **15**	Singgalang **10**	Selamat **6**
Kartini **5**		Simpang Raya **1**

on Wednesday and Saturday (0800-1700) when hordes of Minangkabau men and women descend on Bukittinggi. The market – in fact there are two, the Upper Market (*Pasar Atas*) and Lower Market (*Pasar Bawah*) – covers an enormous area and sells virtually everything. Good for souvenirs, handicrafts, jewellery, fruit, spices and weird foods.

The north end of Jalan Jend A Yani runs between two hills that have recently been linked by a footbridge. On top of the hill to the west is **Fort de Kock**, built by the Dutch in 1825 as a defensive site during the Padri Wars. Very little of the fort remains apart from a few rusting cannon and a moat. The centre of the decaying fortifications is dominated by a water tower. However, the views of the town and the surrounding countryside are worth the trip (although trees are beginning to obscure the view). To the east, and linked by a footbridge, on the other side of Jalan Jend A Yani, is Bukittinggi's high point, **Taman Bundokandung** ('Kind-Hearted Mother Park'). The park contains both a museum and a zoo. The **Bukittinggi Zoo** ⓘ *daily 0730-1700, fort and zoo: 5000Rp (8000Rp on public holidays)*, is hardly a lesson in how to keep animals in captivity, but it does have a reasonable collection of Sumatran wildlife, including orang-utans and gibbons. Within the zoo is a **museum** ⓘ *daily 0730-1700, 1000Rp*, established in 1935 and the oldest in Sumatra. The collection is housed in a traditional *rumah adat*, or Minangkabau clan house, embellished with fine woodcarvings and fronted by two rice barns. The museum specializes in local ethnographic exhibits, including fine jewellery and textiles, and is not very informative. There are also some macabre stuffed and deformed buffalo calves here.

To the southwest of the town is the spectacular **Sianok Canyon**, 4 km long and over 100 m deep. A road at the end of Jalan Teuku Umar leads down through the canyon, past the back entrances to the Japanese tunnel system. A path leaves the road at a sharp bend (there is a snack bar here) and continues to a bridge at the foot of the chasm and steep steps on the opposite side of the canyon. Follow a road through a village and across paddy fields for about two hours until you eventually arrive at **Kota Gadang**. Many small silversmiths sell their wares throughout the village. This is a good place to buy smaller silver items; recommended is **Silversmith Aino** ⓘ *at the coffee shop, Jln Hadisash 115*. There is a large tourist gift centre, **Amai Satia**, in Kota Gadang (walk to the mosque and turn right at the T-junction). From Kota Gadang, either retrace your steps, or head for the crossroads in Kota Gadang where you can catch a blue oplet to Aur Kuning (4000Rp).

Also at the southern edge of town and overlooking the canyon is **Panorama Park** ⓘ *3000Rp (4000Rp on public holidays)*, a popular weekend meeting place for courting couples. Within the park is the entrance to a **maze of tunnels** ⓘ *entrance included in price of entrance ticket to park*, excavated by the Japanese during the Occupation, with ammunition stores, kitchens and dining rooms. Guides gleefully show the chute where dead Indonesian workers were propelled out into the canyon to rot. Opposite the park, on Jalan Panorama (formerly Jalan Imam Bonjol), is the **Army Museum** (**Museum Perjuangan**) ⓘ *daily 0800-1700, 2000Rp (although it looks distinctly under-staffed nowadays)*, which contains military memorabilia from the early 19th century through to the modern period. There are some interesting photographs of the disinterring of the army officers assassinated by the PKI during the attempted coup of 1965.

Around Bukittinggi

One of the attractions of Bukittinggi is the array of sights in the surrounding area. The Minang Highlands around Bukittinggi constitute the core – or *darek* – of the Minang homeland. Below are the main excursions, although there are also additional hikes, waterfalls, traditional villages, lakes and centres of craft production.

Many of the sights and places of interest listed here are under separate headings following the Bukittinggi entry. These are: **Danau Maninjau**, **Payakumbuh** and the **Harau Valley**, **Batusangkar** and **Danau Singkarak**, and **Padang Panjang**. Seeing these sights, particularly if time is short, is easiest on a tour. Getting around the Minang area on public transport is time consuming (renting a motorbike for the day makes for greater mobility).

A guide should, in theory, be able to offer some insights into the rich Minang culture. It is worth asking around and getting some first-hand assessments from travellers who have just returned from tours and who may be able to recommend a guide. If possible, find a guide and arrange a tour directly; the tour companies usually use the same guides and because they take a commission the rate rises. The guides working out of the **Orchid Hotel**, the **Canyon Café** have been recommended. See What to do, page 68.

From Bukittinggi to Maninjau

This trip is spectacular. After leaving the main Padang– Bukittinggi route at Kota Baru, the road twists through the terraced countryside to the town of **Matur**. Locals are said to call this stretch of road the Mercedes Bends, and the story is charming even if it might not be true. During the Dutch period there were two sugar cane processing plants at Matur and the Dutch manager of one owned the only car in the area: a Mercedes. When he drove to Bukittinggi local people would line the road to watch the strange machine wind its way to Kota Baru, earning this stretch of road the name the Mercedes Bends. On reaching the crater lip – an awesome spectacle – the road descends through 44 hairpin bends, each of which has been numbered (and sponsored by a cigarette company) by some bureaucratic mind, before arriving at the lake edge village of Maninjau.

A rewarding and spectacular hike from Bukittinggi, easily possible in a day for even the modestly energetic, is to walk to the crater edge at **Puncak Lawang** (Lawang Top) and then down the steep crater sides to the lake-side village of **Bayur**, before catching a bus back to Bukittinggi. To do this, take a bus from Bukittinggi's Aur Kuning bus terminal to Lawang – sometimes called Pasar Lawang (Lawang Market) to distinguish it from Puncak Lawang (8000Rp). From Lawang walk the 4 km to Puncak Lawang at the lip of the crater and 1400 m up – a spectacular view – before taking the path down (a walk of around another two to three hours). The path can be narrow at times, and slippery when wet. Alternatively, catch a bus straight to Maninjau village on the lake shore, navigating the 44 hairpin bends on the way down (one to two hours, 10,000Rp). The last bus leaves Maninjau village for Bukittinggi between 1600 and 1700, later on market days (Monday to Friday). Check there is no mist before departing.

Danau Singkarak
① *Take a bus heading south towards Solok.*
The Minang area's other lake is Danau Singkarak. It is not as beautiful as Maninjau, but it is possible to come here on a circular journey via Batusangkar.

Batang Palupuh

ⓘ *Catch a bus to Batang Palupuh on the Trans-Sumatran Highway, or take an oplet and then walk to the reserve (30mins).*

This reserve, situated 12 km north of town, is for the monstrous **rafflesia** flower. Ask staff at your guesthouse when the flower will next be in bloom; a guide from the village will point it out for a small fee.

Pandai Sikat and other craft villages

ⓘ *Take a red oplet towards Padang Panjang from the Aur Kuning terminal, get off at Kota Baru and either walk the last 3 km or take an omprengan (a non-licensed bemo) from the intersection.*

One of a number of villages specializing in traditional craft production. Pandai Sikat is situated 13 km south of town at the foot of Mount Singgalang, 3 km off the main road to Padang Panjang, and is a cloth and woodcarving centre. The carvings tend to use natural motifs (trees, animals, flowers, etc), as does the famous *songket* cloth that is produced here. About 1000 women weave richly patterned cloth. Note that the warp may be rayon, imported from Japan, and only the weft, cotton or silk.

Other craft villages include **Desa Sunga**, 17 km south of town, which specializes in brasswork; and **Sungaipua**, on the slopes of Mount Merapi, which specializes in metalwork (knives, swords).

Mount Merapi

ⓘ *Catch a bus to Kota Baru from the Aur Kuning terminal (1st departure 0500), and then hike.*

This active volcano, southeast of town, stands at a height of 2891 m and last erupted in 1979. The difficult climb to the summit takes between four and six hours. Enquire at the Police Station in Kota Baru for more information. Register here before ascending and ask for directions; the route is indistinct in places. The best way to see the volcano is to hire a guide and climb up at night (US$25), arriving at the summit for sunrise and thus avoiding the heat of the day and the mist that envelopes the mountain by 1100. Wear warm clothes as it is cold on the summit. The ground around the crater is loose and hikers should keep away from the lip. Many hotels and cafés can arrange tours and a good place to enquire is at the **Orchid Hotel** or **Canyon Café**. On Saturday nights hoards of locals climb the volcano, following them is possible but not advisable as many do not know the way.

Mount Singgalang

ⓘ *Take an oplet to Kota Baru from the Aur Kuning terminal. From where you are dropped, turn right at the mosque and walk down to Kota Baru. In the centre of the village is a right-hand turn with the RTCI 4 km sign (referring to the radio installation situated 2 km above Pantai Sikat). Follow this track for 2 km to Pandai Sikat. The mountain path starts to the right of the RTCI installation behind a refreshment hut (often closed). For speed, it is possible to hire a motorbike to the RTCI site. Buses back to Bukittinggi run late, but it is advisable not to descend in darkness.*

Singgalang, which lies to the southwest of Bukittinggi, stands at a height of 2878 m and offers a less arduous climb than Mount Merapi. The trail starts at the village of Pandai Sikat, and the climb takes about four or five hours. It's a disappointing dirty footpath. Near the summit, the ground is scree, so good footwear is recommended. Start early, as mist often descends over the mountain later in the day. Tours are available from the **Canyon Café** and **Orchid Guesthouse** for US$25.

Payakumbuh
ⓘ *Regular oplets from Bukittinggi, 1 hr, these run through Piladang.*
This key centre of Minang culture lies about 10 km east of Bukittinggi (see page 58). En route is the colourful local Friday market at **Piladang**, while on the other side of Payakumbuh is the **Harau Canyon** (see below).

Harau Canyon
ⓘ *Take one of the many buses from Bukittinggi to Payakumbuh. From there catch a white oplet – or a 'sago' as they are called locally – running towards Sarialamat to the turn-off for the Harau Valley (see the main entry for more details on the walk from there).*
The canyon lies around 44 km from Bukittinggi, off the road leading through Payakumbuh towards Pekanbaru.

Pariangan and other Minang villages
ⓘ *There are no direct buses from Bukittinggi, catch an oplet from Bukittinggi to Batusangkar, and then one heading towards Kota Baru – which passes through Parianagan. From Bukittinggi it is necessary to first catch an oplet to Batusangkar, and then a Solok-bound bus.*
Pariangan is a peaceful Minang village on the slopes of Mount Merapi. Balimbiang is about 10 km south of Batusangkar, and 1 km off the main road.

Danau Maninjau → *For listings, see pages 65-70.*

Danau Maninjau is one of the most beautiful and impressive natural sights in Sumatra, rivalling Danau Toba. It is a huge, flooded volcanic crater with steep 600-m-high walls. To the west and south the crater walls are largely forested, dropping straight into the lake and leaving scarcely any scope for cultivation and settlement. This part of the crater supports a fair amount of wildlife. To the east and north there is some flat land and this is where Maninjau's small settlements are to be found. Once a popular stop on a jaunt around Sumatra, Maninjau has suffered chronically in the downturn in tourism. Many hotels and restaurants have been forced out of business. If it's tourist-free isolation that you crave, it can be found here in abundance.

Arriving in Danau Maninjau
Regular buses service the route from Bukittinggi, taking 1½ hours. Bicycles and motorcycles can be hired from most guesthouses and provide an ideal means of getting around the lake and reaching surrounding villages. Bicycles cost about US$2-3 per day and motorcycles US$5-6 per day.

Places in Danau Maninjau
The lake offers reasonable swimming (although close to the shore it can be murky), fishing and waterskiing. In 1996, discharges of sulphur from hot underwater springs killed many of the fish that are raised here in cages along the shore. The springs explain why the water is surprisingly warm for a lake over 500 m above sea level.

Maninjau village lies on the east shore of the lake at the point where the road from Bukittinggi reaches the lake. It is a small but booming market and administrative centre. Most of the places to stay are in (and beyond) the northern extent of the village. Around 3 km north of Maninjau village is the small and charming hamlet of **Bayur**. This is quite simply a gem of a community. Most of the houses and other buildings are made of wood or

Maninjau

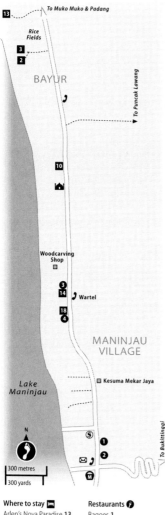

Where to stay 🛏
Arlen's Nova Paradise **13**
Batu C **2**
Maranay Beach **10**
Lily's **3**
Pasir Panjang Permai **14**
Tan Dirih **18**

Restaurants 🍴
Bagoes **1**
Monica's **2**
Nabila **3**
Sambalado **3**
Waterfront Zalino **4**

are white stuccoed brick, and date from the Dutch period. On the northern edge of the village are several more guesthouses, some of the most peaceful in the area. Wandering around Bayur it is easy to imagine what villages were like before individualism and licence destroyed the bonds of community. Continuing further around the lake the road passes through Muko Muko and then onto Lubuk Basung, where the buses terminate. Most buses from Bukittinggi terminate in Lubuk Busung, a few kilometres past Bayur. Tourists who wish to stay in Bayur should inform the driver, and ask to alight at the desired guesthouse.

There are hiking trails through the surrounding countryside. Because the village is some 500 m above sea level, it is cool even during the day and can be chilly at night.

Around Danau Maninjau

From Maninjau village, a worthwhile walk or bicycle ride is around the north edge of the lake to the village of **Muko Muko**, 16 km in all (buses also ply the route). Just before Muko Muko there are the **Alamada Hot Springs** (rather small and insignificant), an excellent fish restaurant and a hydropower station. The total distance around the lake is about 50 km: 20 km on a good road; 30 km on a dirt track. Bicycles can be hired from many of the guesthouses and coffee shops (US$2-3 per day).

It is also possible to hike up to, or down from, **Lawang Top (Puncak Lawang)**, on the crater lip. The trail to the crater edge begins in the middle of Bayur, 3 km north of Maninjau village.

Bukittinggi and around listings

For hotel and restaurant price codes and other relevant information, see pages 8-10.

🛏 Where to stay

Bukittinggi *p58, map p59*
Most of the travellers' hotels and guesthouses are concentrated along the north end of Jln Jend A Yani. Quieter, smaller and often cleaner homestays are located on the hills either side of Jln Jend A Yani. The downturn in tourism has meant that a lot of hotels have not been well maintained, and so tourists tend to congregate in the same few places.

Board and lodging in return for English conversation lessons is offered in the town of Batu Sangkar, 1 hr from Bukittinggi. Teaching duties are for 3 hrs a day. Contact Mr Edy at **Family International English School (FIES)**, T0752 71099 or T081 2672 1599. The length of stay is negotiable.
$$$ The Hills, Jln Laras Datuk Bandaro, T0752 35000, www.thehillsbukittinggi.com. This large hotel has a definite North African feel, with its arched entrance, Moroccan fountains and huge atrium. Rooms are a bit of a shock, with bright mint green colour scheme and fairly old furniture. All come with bath, hot water and TV. The de luxe rooms have views of the hills. Pool and spa service. No discounts, but a longer stay gets a room upgrade.
$$$-$$ Hotel Lima's, Jln Kesehatan 35, T0752 22641. This place is popular with Indonesian tour groups and has a range of rooms in concrete blocks on a hillside. Superior rooms are carpeted and have hot water, bath, TV and a range of complimentary goodies. The cheaper rooms are fronted by a small garden, and have TV and hot water.
$$$-$$ Royal Denai Hotel, Jln Dr A Rivai 26, T0752 32920, www.royaldenaihotel. com. Sprawling 3-star hotel crowned with

a Minangkabau roof. Rooms are clean. The cheapest are a bit tatty. Discounts available.
$$ Hotel Benteng, Jln Benteng 1, T0752 21115, www.bentenghotel.com. Perched on a hilltop next to the fort, the rooms have superb views and sizeable hot-water bathrooms. Discounts.
$$-$ The Gallery, Jln H Agus Salim 25, T0752 23515. The de luxe rooms are nothing special, and have soft beds and average views. The economy rooms have a lovely sun terrace with marvellous views.
$$-$ Hotel Asia, Jln Kesehatan 38, T0752 625277. The large reception area is combined with a comfortable Chinese-inspired lobby, and makes for a nice spot for a morning tea. De luxe rooms are spacious and have balcony with exceptional views over the town and to the mountains beyond. Cheaper rooms have shared bathroom but still have good views, some with access to a roof terrace. Recommended.
$ Hotel Dahlia, Jln A Yani 106, T0752 627296, osrina@yahoo.com. Well run, with hot-water rooms, but low on atmosphere. The pricier rooms have access to a roof terrace with good views; the cheaper rooms downstairs are dark. Breakfast is included.
$ Hotel Kartini, Jln Teuku Umar 6, T0752 22885. Homely hotel offering spotless rooms with TV and hot water. The more expensive rooms downstairs are next to the lobby and can be quite noisy. The rooms upstairs are quiet and very comfortable. Ask for the room at the front with a balcony. Recommended.
$ Hotel Singgalang, Jln A Yani 130, T0752 628709. Rooms are clean but have no natural light. All have TV, the slightly more expensive ones have hot-water showers.
$ Merdeka Homestay, Jln Dr A Rivai 20, T0752 23937. Large rooms with attached bathroom (cold water) in a villa near a busy intersection. Can be a little noisy.

$ Minang International Hotel, Jln Panorama 20A, T0752 21120. Soeharto stayed here in 1978, and it seems that little has changed since then. With green and purple carpets, kitsch furniture and peeling wallpaper, this place appeals to a niche audience.

$ Orchid Hotel, Jln Teuku Umar 11, T0752 32634. Currently the most popular cheap place in town, and deservedly so. Rooms are clean, the staff are courteous and helpful. Ask for a room on the side away from the mosque, if you don't want to be disturbed by the call to prayer. Recommended.

Danau Maninjau *p63, map p64*
There are 2 concentrations of guesthouses, in Maninjau village and Bayur, both on the eastern shore. Most places stand empty, and haven't been touched up for years. This is especially noticeable in the cheaper places.

$$-$ Pasir Panjang Permai, T0752 61111. Selection of a/c and non-a/c rooms in 2 concrete blocks. This hotel is geared towards Indonesian tour groups, and gets busy at weekends. More expensive rooms have TV, bath and good views from the balcony. Furniture is a little tatty. Discounts available.

$ Maransay Beach, halfway between Maninjau village and Bayur, T0752 61264. Large wooden hotel built out over the water, with a good restaurant and collection of simple rooms. The ones at the front have a decent amount of natural light. Some rooms have an outside bathroom. There is a small beach beside the hotel. Friendly staff.

$ Tan Dirih, T0752 61461. Tidy, spotless rooms with TV and comfy beds. The large veranda has fine views, and there is free use of tubes here for a day of floating in the lake. You can eat here, but meals need to be ordered well in advance. Recommended.

Bayur
There are fewer places to stay in Bayur than in Maninjau village, although north of the

village is a group of 3 peaceful guesthouses down a series of tracks that run from the road, through ricefields, to the lake, where there is a small beach. These guesthouses are the most peaceful; they are also some distance (3 km) from the main concentration of restaurants and coffee shops. Bemos into and out of Maninjau village stop at 1900, but the walk is beautiful and not far. Try not to arrive here at night, as negotiating the paths through the rice fields in the dark isn't much fun.

$ Arlen Nova's Paradise, T081 5352 04714, www.nova-maninjau.id.or.id. Collection of 5 clean bungalows with attached bathroom set in pleasant garden with lake views.

$ Batu C, next to Lily's. If there is ever an overspill from **Lily's**, this place might get busy. Simple wooden chalets on the lake.

$ Lily's, T081 3749 01435. The most popular guesthouse around the lake, although still very quiet. Rooms are very simple with shared bathroom. The front ones have excellent views. Staff are friendly and cook up some of the best *nasi goreng* with *tempe* in Sumatra. There is a stony swimming area and a small library of books. Recommended.

Restaurants

Bukittinggi *p58, map p59*
Bukittinggi is renowned for the quality of its food. The climate means that temperate as well as tropical vegetables are available. The number of tourist-oriented cafés has decreased over the last few years, but there are more than enough to cater for the small number of visitors. There are also excellent local restaurants serving Minang/Padang and Chinese dishes, and plenty of foodstalls selling *sate*, *gulai* soup and other specialities.

$ Bedual Café, Jln A Yani 95, T0752 31533. Daily 0800-2300. Chilled music and walls covered in eclectic art, this eatery has plenty of Indonesian and Western food including a roast chicken dinner for 2, a dream for those arriving from the hinterlands. Internet is available for 5000Rp per hr. Recommended.

$ Canyon Café, Jln Teuku Umar 8, T0752 21652. Daily 0700-2300. Popular travellers' hang-out with a friendly atmosphere and staff offering good local information. The menu is packed with cheap Western food.

$ Family, Jln Benteng 1. Daily 0700-2100. Superb views and good Indonesian food, the house special is *ikan baker* (grilled fish).

$ La Mor Resto, Jln Dr A Rivai 18, T0752 33800. Daily 0700-2100. This popular student hang-out has a long menu of Indonesian dishes such as *nasi goreng* and *soto ayam* and good cold juices.

$ Mona Lisa, Jln A Yani 58, T0752 22644. Daily 0900-2130. Over the years, this place has decreased in size but still serves up fair portions of Chinese food. The best thing here is the create-your-own tropical fruit salad.

$ Selamat, Jln A Yani 19, T0752 22959. Daily 0600-2100. One of the town's better *nasi Padang* places.

$ Simpang Raya, Jln Minangkabau 77, T0752 21910. Daily 0500-2100. With branches all over town, this chain churns out *nasi Padang* to hungry crowds all day. In the evening it is better to arrive earlier: the later it gets the more the selection diminishes.

Foodstalls
The best ones are all in and around the market area; *sate*, fruit, Padang dishes, etc.

Danau Maninjau *p63, map p64*
There are several good coffee shops geared to Western tastes in Maninjau village, as well as the usual *warungs* and stalls, concentrated in the market area. Many of the guesthouses offer simple meals. **Maransy** and **Lily's ($)** have the most comprehensive menus and are worth trying. There are lots of roadside stalls serving *otak-otak* (minced fish with spices grilled in a banana leaf – delicious).

$ Bagoes, T0752 61418. Daily 0800-2200. Simple menu of Western and Asian food. Run by John who offers good local information. Internet available, 10,000Rp per hr.

$ Monica Café, T0752 61879. Daily 0800-2200. Quiet eatery with occasional movie screenings. Pancakes, juices and comfy chairs. Internet available, 20,000Rp per hr.

$ Nabila. Daily 0800-2000. Fresh grilled lake fish and simple Indonesian standards.

$ Sambalado, T0752 61020. Daily 0700-2000. Big plates of *nasi Padang*.

$ Waterfront Zalino, T0752 61740. Daily 0800-2200. This clean place is a bit of an anomaly for the area, with well-tended lawns, a spotless interior and a lovely pavilion over the water. There is also a kids' pool, and lots of good local information available. The food is simple Western and Indonesian.

⊕ Entertainment

Bukittinggi *p58, map p59*
Minangkabau dances
Dancing, including *Pencak silat*, a traditional form of self-defence, can be seen performed at **Medan Nan Balindung**, Jln Khatib Suleiman 1, Fri-Wed 2030, 40,000Rp.

Minangkabau traditional arts
Music, song, dance and *silat* at **Saayun Salankah**, Jln Lenggogeni 1A, Fri-Sat 2030, 40,000Rp.

O Shopping

Bukittinggi *p58, map p59*
Bukittinggi has a good selection of shops selling handicrafts, curios and antiques, and has a particular reputation for its silver and gold jewellery. The shops are concentrated on Jln Minangkabau (close to the Central Market) and along Jln Jend A Yani and Jln Teuku Umar. The most enjoyable way to shop is in the **central market** on Wed or Sat (see page 59). At other times it mainly sells products for local consumption – lots of clothes, fruit and vegetables,

plastic trinkets, metal goods, fish, dried and otherwise, and so on.

Antiques and curios There is comparatively little for sale that originates from the area around Bukittinggi; most articles are from Nias and Mentawi, from the Batak areas around Danau Toba, and from further afield, like Kalimantan and Java. The art from Nias and Mentawi is easy to fake and it is likely that much on sale is neither old nor genuine – despite the appearance of authenticity that dust may give. Shops include: **Aladdin**, Jln Jend A Yani 14; **Ganesha**, Jln Teuku Umar 2; **Makmar**, Jln Jend A Yani 10 and **Tanjung Raya Art Shop**, Jln Jend A Yani 85.

Handicrafts There are the handicraft villages like Pandai Sikat, as well as a number of shops in town. Many of the antique shops are really jumped-up handicraft outlets. A place with better goods than most is **Sulaman Silungkang** on Jln Panorama.

Jewellery If interested in buying jewellery, it is worth visiting the Kota Gadang silversmithing village (see page 60), which specializes in producing silver filigree.

⊙ What to do

Bukittinggi *p58, map p59*
Buffalo fights
Buffalo fights in the villages around Kota Baru, 10 km to the south of Bukittinggi, have been banned in West Sumatra due to gambling. Ask at your guesthouse.

Rafting
There used to be regular rafting trips down the Batang Anai River and the Sri Antokan rapids, which both flow from Danau Maninjau through the Ngarai Sianok Gorge to Palupuh, and along the Ombilin River that flows out of Danau Singkarak. However,

due to a lack of numbers these have been suspended. Enquire at the **Orchid Hotel**.

Rock climbing
In the late 1990s, Bukittinggi began to gain a reputation for the quality of its rock climbing and its rock climbers. Again, the downturn in tourism, and the fact that the local organizer of trips moved to the USA has meant that they are no longer offered. For independent climbers, it might be possible to get a guide from the **Canyon Café** or **Orchid Hotel**. Climbers will need their own equipment, and bear in mind the danger of attempting such climbs without local knowledge.

Baso is a limestone tower around 10 km due east of Bukittinggi, with a number of challenging routes (Australian grading) including Power Pancake (graded 5.12c), Bee Attack (5.11b), Priest (5.10b), Koorong Bana (5.12d) and Bastard (5.12c). The Harau Canyon (see page 63) offers around 24 routes including the technically demanding Liang Limbek (5.13a).

Swimming
The **Hills**' romantic Romanesque heated pool is open to non-residents, Mon-Fri 25,000Rp, Sat-Sun 30,000Rp, 2000Rp for children. If you have lunch at the hotel they will allow you to swim for free.

Tour operators
Tour companies are concentrated along Jln Jend A Yani. They can reconfirm flights and provide bus tickets, also organize local tours and tours further afield.
Maju Indosari Travel Bureau, Jln Muka Jam Gadang 17, T0752 21671.
Raun Sumatra, Jln A Yani 99, T0752 21133. Professional outfit.
Tigo Balai, Jln A Yani 100, T0752 627235.

Tours
Local tours There are a range of tours organized to Danau Maninjau, Batusangkar, Danau Singkarak and other sights around

Bukittinggi. Tours tend to take 1 of 3 routes: the Minangkabau tour, featuring many different places that are representative of the Minangkabau culture, past and present (including Batusangkar, Pagaruyung and Danau Singkarak). Secondly, the Maninjau line (including Kota Gadang and Danau Maninjau), and finally, the Harau Valley line (including Mount Merapi and the Harau Valley). Most tour/travel agents organize these day-long tours for US$7-15; they are also arranged by many hotels and guesthouses.

Tours further afield Many of the tour operators also organize tours further afield, for example, 10-day trips to the Mentawai Islands. Bukittinggi is an excellent place to arrange a tour to the islands off the West Sumatra coast, but bear in mind that it can take up to 3 days to get to Siberut Island, Mentawai. Again, ask fellow travellers for feedback regarding guides. Expect to pay around US$300 for an 8- to 10-day all-inclusive trip to the islands.

Danau Maninjau *p63, map p64*
Tour operators
Kesuma Mekar Jaya, T0752 61300. Offers tours around the region, but they are more expensive than those on offer in Bukittinggi. Door-to-door minibuses can be organized from here, every 2 hrs to Padang, 60,000Rp. Money-changing service and flight ticketing.

⊖ Transport

Bukittinggi *p58, map p59*
Air
Given the cheap price of flying in Indonesia, many people fly out of Padang Minangkabau International Airport to Medan or Jakarta rather than facing the Trans-Sumatran Highway. Flights can be booked at all travel agencies in town, and **Raun Sumatra** and **Tigo Balai** (see Tour operators) have shuttle buses to the airport from Bukittinggi for 35,000Rp.

Bus
Local The station is at Aur Kuning, 3 km southeast of town. Buses to local destinations including **Batusangkar** (8000Rp), **Maninjau** (10,000Rp), **Payakumbuh** (8000Rp) and **Padang** (15,000Rp). There are also buses to destinations further afield.

Long distance For **Parapat**, choose the bus company carefully as many people have been overcharged; ensure that you have a ticket with seat numbers. Note that the bus may not connect with the last ferry to **Samosir** (1830), which means a late-night arrival at Parapat and a limited choice of hotels. Also, ensure that your bus is travelling to Parapat, rather than **Pematangsiantar**, as there have been some problems with the roads around Toba. Tickets are also available from travel agents and guesthouses. The Orchid Hotel (see Where to stay) is a reliable place and has tickets for a/c express bus to Parapat for US$19 (including transfer to bus station).

ANS, T0752 22626, and ALS, T0752 21214, offices at bus terminal, have a/c buses to **Parapat**, 15 hrs, US$22; **Medan**, 20 hrs, US$22; **Jakarta**, 30 hrs, US$38; **Pekanbaru**, 6 hrs, US$6.50; and **Bandung**, 36 hrs; US$41.

Taxi
Taxis can be hired, even as far as Medan. Ask at one of the tour offices (see above).

Danau Maninjau *p63, map p64*
Air
To reach Padang Minangkabau International Airport, there is a door-to-door minibus service offered by **Raun Sumatra** and **Tigo Balai** (see Tour operators) in Bukittinggi for 35,000Rp. DAMRI buses meet each arriving plane and shuttle passengers to **Padang** or **Bukittinggi** for 15,000Rp.

Domestic To **Batam**, daily with Mandala; **Jakarta**, daily with Lion Air, Mandala, Sriwijaya and Garuda; **Medan**, daily with

Mandala. Tickets can be booked at travel agencies in Bukittinggi and Padang.
International Singapore, Tue, Thu, Sat, Tiger Airways. **Kuala Lumpur**, daily with AirAsia.

Bus

Regular buses from Bukittinggi to **Maninjau** village, negotiating 44 bends down from the crater lip to the lake, 1½ hrs, 10,000Rp. Buses also continue on through Bayur to **Muko Muko** on the northwest side of the lake. Those wishing to get back to Bukittinggi need to wait at the road near the entrance to their hotel and flag down a bus from Lubuk Basung to Bukittinggi via Maninjau village. The last bus to Bukittinggi leaves around 1700. From Padang catch a bus to Bukittinggi and ask to be let off at Kuto Tuo, the turn-off for Maninjau, and wait there to catch a bus down to the lake. There is a daily bus to **Pekanbaru**, 7 hrs, 60,000Rp.

Oplets

Some oplets from Bukittinggi continue anti-clockwise around the lake through Bayur and Muko Muko to Lubuk Basung (3000Rp), the end of the road, so to speak.

● Directory

Bukittinggi *p58, map p59*
Banks Banks close at 1100 on Sat. Many tour and travel companies change money. Bank Negara Indonesia, Jln Jend A Yani, changes TCs. Bank Rakyat Indonesia, Jln Jend A Yani 3. PT Enzet Corindo Perkasa, Jln Minangkabau 51 (money changer).
Internet Bedual Café. **Medical services** Dokter Achmad Mochtar Hospital, Jln Rivai (opposite the Denai Hotel). **Post office** Jln Kemerdekaan, on the south edge of town; the 2 bookshops on Jln Jend A Yani in the centre of town sell stamps and have post boxes; Branch Post Office, Clock Tower Square.
Telephone Wartel office, Jln Jend A Yani, for international calls and faxes.

Danau Maninjau *p63, map p64*
Banks Bank Rakyat Indonesia, Jln SMP (short distance north of the bus stop in the centre of town). **Medical services** Clinic at the southern end of Maninjau village.
Post office Jln Muara Pisang (facing police station, not far from oplet stop).
Telephone Jln SMP (facing oplet stop in town), international calls can be made from the office.

Background

Pre-colonial history

Unlike the states of mainland Southeast Asia, which did enjoy a certain geographical legitimacy prior to the colonial period, Indonesia was a fragmented assemblage of kingdoms, sultanates, principalities and villages. It is true that there was a far greater degree of communication and intercourse than many assume, so that no part of the archipelago can be treated in isolation, but nonetheless, it is still difficult to talk of 'Indonesian' history prior to the 19th century.

The great empires of the pre-colonial period did range beyond their centres of power, but none came close to controlling all the area now encompassed by the modern Indonesian state. Among these empires, the most powerful were the Srivijayan Kingdom based at Palembang in South Sumatra; and the great Javanese Dynasties of Sailendra, Majapahit and Mataram. There was also a string of less powerful, but nonetheless influential, kingdoms; for example, the Sultanate of Aceh in North Sumatra, the Gowa Kingdom of South Sulawesi, the trading sultanates of the Spice Islands of Maluku, and the Hindu kingdoms of Bali. The history of each of these powers is dealt with in the appropriate regional introduction.

Even after the European powers arrived in the archipelago, their influence was often superficial. They were concerned only with controlling the valuable spice trade, and were not inclined to feats of territorial expansion. To get around this lack of a common history, historians tend to talk instead in terms of common processes of change. The main ones affecting the archipelago were the 'Indianization' of the region from the 1st century AD and the introduction of Hinduism and Buddhism; the arrival of Islam in North Sumatra in the 13th century and then its spread east and south during the 15th century; and the contrast between inwardly-focused agricultural kingdoms and outwardly orientated trading states.

Colonial history

During the course of the 15th century, the two great European maritime powers of the time, Spain and Portugal, were exploring sea routes to the east. Two forces were driving this search: the desire for profits, and the drive to evangelize. At the time, even the wealthy in Europe had to exist on pickled and salted fish and meat during the winter months (fodder crops for winter feed were not grown until the 18th century). Spices to flavour what would otherwise be a very monotonous diet were greatly sought after and commanded a high price. This was not just a passing European fad. An Indian Hindu wrote that: "When the palate revolts against the insipidness of rice boiled with no other ingredients, we dream of fat, salt and spices".

Of the spices, cloves and nutmeg originated from just one location, the Moluccas (Maluku) – the Spice Islands of eastern Indonesia. Perhaps because of their value, spices and their places of origin were accorded mythical status in Europe. The 14th century French friar Catalani Jordanus claimed, for example, that the clove flowers of Java produced an odour so strong it killed "every man who cometh among them, unless he shut his mouth and nostrils".

It was in order to break the monopoly on the spice trade held by Venetian and Muslim Arab traders that the Portuguese began to extend their possessions eastwards. This finally culminated in the capture of the port of Melaka by the Portuguese seafarer Alfonso de Albuquerque in June 1511. The additional desire to spread the Word of God is clear in the speech that Albuquerque made before the battle with the Muslim sultan of Melaka, when he exhorted his men, stressing: "... the great service which we shall perform to our Lord in casting the Moors out of this country and of quenching the fire of the sect of Mohammet so that it may never burst out again hereafter".

From their base in Melaka, the Portuguese established trading relations with the Moluccas, and built a series of forts across the region: at Bantam (Banten), Flores, Ternate, Tidore, Timor and Ambon (Amboyna).

Many accounts of Indonesian history treat the arrival of the Portuguese Admiral Alfonso de Albuquerque off Malacca (Melaka) in 1511, and the dispatch of a small fleet to the Spice Islands, as a watershed in Indonesian history. As the historian MC Ricklefs argues, this view is untenable, writing that "... in the early years of the Europeans' presence, their influence was sharply limited in both area and depth".

The Portuguese only made a significant impact in the Spice Islands, leaving their mark in a number of Indonesian words of Portuguese origin – for example, *sabun* (soap), *meja* (table) and *Minggu* (Sun). They also introduced Christianity to East Indonesia and disrupted the islands' prime export – spices. But it was the Dutch, in the guise of the **Vereenigde Oost-Indische Compagnie** or **VOC** (the Dutch East India Company), who began the process of western intrusion. They established a toehold in Java – which the Portuguese had never done – a precursor to later territorial expansion. But this was a slow process and it was not until the early 20th century – barely a generation before the Japanese occupation – that the Dutch could legitimately claim they held administrative authority over the whole country.

The idea of Indonesia, 1900-1942

The beginning of the 20th century marks a turning point in Indonesian history. As Raden Kartini, a young educated Javanese woman, wrote in a letter dated 12 January 1900: "Oh, it is splendid just to live in this age; the transition of the old into the new!". It was in 1899 that the Dutch lawyer C Th van Deventer published a ground-breaking paper entitled *Een eereschuld* or 'A debt of honour'. This article argued that having exploited the East Indies for so long, and having extracted so much wealth from the colony, it was time for the Dutch government to restructure their policies and focus instead on improving conditions for Indonesians. In 1901, the Ethical Policy – as it became known – was officially embraced. Van Deventer was commissioned to propose ways to further such a policy and suggested a formulation of 'education, irrigation and emigration'. The Ethical Policy represented a remarkable change in perspective, but scholars point out that it was very much a creation of the European mind and made little sense in Indonesian terms.

The Indonesian economy was also changing in character. The diffusion of the cash economy through the islands and the growing importance of export crops like rubber and coffee, and minerals such as tin and oil, were transforming the country. Christianity, too, became a powerful force for change, particularly in the islands beyond Muslim Java. There was large-scale conversion in central and North Sulawesi, Flores, among the Batak of Sumatra, in Kalimantan, and Timor. In response to the inroads that Christianity was making in the Outer Islands, Islam in Java became more orthodox and reformist. The 'corrupt' *abangan*, who adhered to what has become known as the 'Javanese religion' – a mixture of Muslim, Hindu, Buddhist and animist beliefs – were gradually displaced by the stricter *santris*.

At about the same time, there was an influx of *trekkers*, or Dutch expatriates, who came to the East Indies with their wives and Dutch cultural perspectives, with the intention of going 'home' after completing their contracts. They overwhelmed the older group of *blijvers* or 'stayers', and there emerged a more racist European culture, one that denigrated *Indische* culture and extolled the lifestyle of the Dutch. The Chinese community, like the Dutch, was also divided into two groups: the older immigrants or *peranakan* who had assimilated into Indies culture, and the more recent *totok* arrivals who zealously maintained their culture, clinging to their Chinese roots.

So, the opening years of the 20th century presented a series of paradoxes. On the one hand, Dutch policy was more sensitive to the needs of the 'natives'; yet many Dutch were becoming less understanding of Indonesian culture and more bigoted. At the same time, while the Chinese and Dutch communities were drawing apart from the native Indonesians and into distinct communities based upon Chinese and European cultural norms, so the economy was becoming increasingly integrated and international. Perhaps inevitably, tensions arose, and these began to mould the social and political landscape of confrontation between the colonialists and the natives.

A number of political parties and pressure groups emerged from this maelstrom of forces. In 1912, a Eurasian – one of those who found himself ostracized from European-colonial culture – EFE Douwes Dekker founded the Indies Party. This was a revolutionary grouping with the slogan 'the Indies for those who make their home there'. In the same year, a batik merchant from Surakarta established the Sarekat Islam or 'Islamic Union', which quickly became a mass organization under the leadership of the charismatic orator HOS Cokroaminoto. Seven years later it had over 2,000,000 members. In 1914, a small group of *totok* Dutch immigrants founded the Indies Social-Democratic Association in Semarang. Finally, in 1920, the Perserikatan Komunis di India (PKI) or the Indies Communist Party was established.

In 1919, the Dutch colonial authorities decided to clamp down on all dissent. The flexibility that had characterized Dutch policy until then was abandoned in favour of an increasingly tough approach. But despite the rounding-up of large numbers of subversives, and the demise of the PKI and emasculation of the Sarekat Islam, it was at this time that the notion of 'Indonesia' first emerged. In July 1927, Sukarno founded the Partai Nasional Indonesia or PNI. In October 1928, a Congress of Indonesian Youth coined the phrase 'one nation – Indonesia, one people – Indonesian, one language – Indonesian'. At the same congress the Indonesian flag was designed and the Indonesian national anthem sung for the first time – *Indonesia Raya*. As John Smail writes in the book *In Search of Southeast Asia*:

"The idea of Indonesia spread so easily, once launched, that it seemed to later historians as if it had always existed, if not actually explicitly then inchoate in the hearts of the people. But it was, in fact, a new creation, the product of a great and difficult leap of the imagination. The idea of Indonesia required the denial of the political meaning of the societies into which the first Indonesians had been born".

In spite of Dutch attempts to stifle the nationalist spirit, it spread through Indonesian, and particularly Javanese, society. By 1942, when the Japanese occupied the country, the idea of Indonesia as an independent nation was firmly rooted.

The Japanese occupation, 1942-1945

Although the Japanese occupation lasted less than four years, it fundamentally altered the forces driving the country towards independence. Prior to 1942, the Dutch faced no real challenge to their authority; after 1945, it was only a question of time before independence. The stunning victory of the Japanese in the Dutch East Indies destroyed the image of colonial invincibility, undermined the prestige of the Dutch among many

Indonesians, and – when the Dutch returned to power after 1945 – created an entirely new psychological relationship between rulers and ruled.

But the Japanese were not liberators. Their intention of creating a Greater East Asia Co-Prosperity Sphere did not include offering Indonesians independence. They wished to control Indonesia for their own interests. The Japanese did give a certain latitude to nationalist politicians in Java, but only as a means of mobilizing Indonesian support for their war effort. Sukarno and Muhammad Hatta were flown to Tokyo in November 1943 and decorated by Emperor Hirohito. For the Dutch and their allies, the war meant incarceration. There were 170,000 internees, including 60,000 women and children. About a quarter died in captivity.

One particularly sordid side of the occupation which has come to light in recent years is the role of 'comfort women'. This euphemism should be more accurately translated as 'sex slaves' – women who were forced to satisfy the needs of Japanese soldiers to aid the war effort. For years the Japanese government denied such comfort stations existed, but documents unearthed in Japan have indicated beyond doubt that they were very much part of the war infrastructure. Much of the attention has focused upon comfort women from Korea, China and the Philippines, but there were also stations in Indonesia. These women, so long cowed and humiliated into silence, are now talking about their experiences to force the Japanese government to accept responsibility. Dutch-Australian Jan Ruff is one of these brave women. A young girl living in Java before the war, she was interned in Camp Ambarawa with her mother and two sisters. In February 1944 she was taken, along with nine other girls, to a brothel in Semarang for the sexual pleasure of Japanese officers. In her testimony at a public meeting in Tokyo in December 1992 she recounted: "During that time [at the brothel] the Japanese had abused me and humiliated me. They had ruined my young life. They had stripped me of everything, my self-esteem, my dignity, my freedom, my possessions, my family." Belatedly, the Japanese government offered its 'sincere apologies and remorse' in August 1993, 48 years afterwards. The fact that the apology came on the last day of the Liberal Democratic Party's government detracted from the honesty of the remarks. Many still feel that Japanese leaders find it difficult to be sincere about events almost half a century old.

As the Japanese military lost ground in the Pacific to the advancing Americans, so their rule over Indonesia became increasingly harsh. Peasants were forcibly recruited as 'economic soldiers' to help the war effort – about 75,000 died – and the Japanese were even firmer in their suppression of dissent than the Dutch had been before them. But as the military situation deteriorated, the Japanese gradually came to realize the necessity of allowing nationalist sentiments greater rein. On 7 September 1944, Prime Minister Koiso promised independence, and in March 1945 the creation of an Investigating Committee for Preparatory Work for Indonesian Independence was announced. Among its members were Sukarno, Hatta and Muhammad Yamin. On 1 June, Sukarno mapped out his philosophy of Pancasila or Five Principles which were to become central tenets of independent Indonesia. On 15 August, after the second atomic bomb was dropped on Nagasaki, the Japanese unconditionally surrendered. Sukarno, Hatta and the other independence leaders now had to act quickly before the Allies helped the Dutch re-establish control. On 17 August 1945, Sukarno read out the Declaration of Independence, Indonesia's red and white flag was raised and a small group of onlookers sang the national anthem, Indonesia Raya.

Revolutionary struggle, 1945-1950
In September 1945, the first units of the British Army landed at Jakarta to re-impose Dutch rule. They arrived to find an Indonesian administration already in operation. Confrontation was inevitable. Young Indonesians responded by joining the revolutionary struggle, which

became known as the Pemuda Movement (*pemuda* means youth). This reached its height between 1945 and mid-1946, and brought together young men and women of all classes, binding them together in a common cause. The older nationalists found themselves marginalized in this increasingly violent and fanatical response. Men like Sukarno and Hatta adopted a policy of *diplomasi* – negotiating with the Dutch. The supporters of the Pemuda Movement embraced *perjuangan* – the armed struggle. Not only the Dutch, but also minorities like the Chinese, Eurasians and Ambonese, suffered from atrocities at the hands of the Pemuda supporters. The climax of the Pemuda Movement came in November 1945 with the battle for Surabaya.

In 1947, the Dutch were militarily strong enough to regain control of Java, and East and South Sumatra. At the end of 1948, a second thrust of this 'Police Action' re-established control over much of the rest of the country. Ironically, these military successes played an important role in the final 'defeat' of the Dutch in Indonesia. They turned the United Nations against Holland, forcing the Dutch government to give way over negotiations. On 2 November the Hague Agreement was signed, paving the way for full political independence of all former territories of the Dutch East Indies (with the exception of West Irian) on 27 December 1949.

From independence to Guided Democracy to coup: 1950-1965

In 1950, Indonesia was an economic shambles and in political chaos. Initially, there was an attempt to create a political system based on the western European model of parliamentary democracy. By 1952 the futility of expecting a relatively painless progression to this democratic ideal was becoming obvious, despite the holding of a parliamentary general election in 1955 with a voter turnout of over 90%. Conflicts between Communists, radical Muslims, traditional Muslims, regional groups and minorities led to a series of coups, rebel governments and violent confrontations. Indonesia was unravelling and in the middle of 1959, President Sukarno cancelled the provisional constitution and introduced his period of Guided Democracy.

This period of relative political stability rested on an alliance between the army, the Communist PKI, and Sukarno himself. It was characterized by extreme economic nationalism, with assets controlled by Dutch, British and Indian companies and individuals being expropriated. The **Konfrontasi** with the Dutch over the 'recovery' of West Irian from 1960 to 1962, and with Malaysia over Borneo beginning in 1963, forced Sukarno to rely on Soviet arms shipments, and Indonesia moved increasingly into the Soviet sphere of influence. Cracks between the odd alliance of PKI and the army widened, and even Sukarno's popular support and force of character could not stop the dam from bursting. On 1 October 1965, six senior generals were assassinated by a group of middle-ranking officers, thus ending the period of Guided Democracy. MC Ricklefs writes: "... on that night the balance of hostile forces which underlay guided democracy came to an end. Many observers have seen tragedy in the period, especially in the tragedy of Sukarno, the man who outlived his time and used his popular support to maintain a regime of extravagant corruption and hypocrisy."

The coup was defeated by the quick-thinking of General Suharto whose forces overcame those of the coup's leaders. However, it undermined both Sukarno and the PKI as both were linked with the plot – the former by allowing the PKI to gain such influence, and the latter by allegedly master-minding the coup. Most Indonesians, although not all western academics, see the coup as a Communist plot hatched by the PKI with the support of Mao Zedong and the People's Republic of China. It led to massacres on a huge scale as bands of youths set about exterminating those who were thought to be PKI supporters. This was supported, implicitly, by the army and there were news reports of 'streams choked with bodies'. The reaction was most extreme in Java and Bali, but there were murders across the archipelago. The number killed is not certain; estimates vary from 100,000 to 1,000,000 and the true figure probably lies somewhere between the two (500,000 is widely quoted). In Bali alone some scholars believe that 80,000 people died – around 5% of the population. The difficulty is that the body count kept by the military is widely regarded as a gross under-estimate. Oei Tjoe Tat, a cabinet minister under Sukarno, was sent on a fact-finding mission to discover the scale of the massacres. He calculated that by January 1966 500,000 people had died. The military's figure at that time was 80,000. As it was an anti-Communist purge, and as China had been blamed for fermenting the coup, many of those killed were Chinese who were felt, by their mere ethnicity, to have leftist-inclinations and Communist sympathies. Few doubt that the majority were innocent traders and middlemen, whose economic success and ethnic origin made them scapegoats. Islamic clerics and members of youth groups seem to have been particularly instrumental in singling out people for extermination. While these uncontrolled massacres were occurring, power was transferred to General Suharto (although he was not elected president until 1968). This marked the shift from what has become known as the Old Order, to the New Order.

That the events of 1965 remain contentious is reflected in the government's attempts to re-write, and in places to erase, this small slice of history. In 1995, three decades after the events of 1965-1966, the authorities banned Oei Tjoe Tat's autobiography *Oei Tjoe Tat: assistant to President Sukarno*. It seems that the account of the anti-communist purge diverged too much from the official history. The fact that banned novelist and former political prisoner Pramoedya Ananta Toer had a hand in the book also cannot have endeared it to the authorities. By the time it was banned, however, around 15,000 copies had already been sold. Documents relating to the 1965-1996 upheaval are restricted, and instead the government produces its own sanitized version of events. This has it that the Communists were behind the attempted coup, that President Sukarno was misguided in allowing the Communists to gain so much power, and that only the quick-thinking and courageous military, with Suharto at the fore, thwarted the attempt and saved Indonesia from turmoil.

Political and economic developments under the New Order: 1965 to present

When Suharto took power in 1965 he had to deal with an economy in disarray. There was hyper-inflation, virtually no inward investment and declining productivity. To put the economy back on the rails, he turned to a group of US-trained economists who became known as the Berkeley Mafia. They recommended economic reform, the return of expropriated assets, and a more welcoming political and economic climate for foreign investment. In terms of international relations, Suharto abandoned the policy of support for China and the Soviet Union and moved towards the western fold. Diplomatic relations with China were severed (and only renewed in 1990), and the policy of confrontation against Malaysia brought to an end.

The 33 years from 1965 through to 1998 was one of political stability. Suharto stayed in power for over three decades, and he presided over a political system which in a number of respects had more in common with the Dutch era than with that of former President Sukarno. Suharto eschewed ideology as a motivating force, kept a tight control of administration, and attempted to justify his leadership by offering his people economic well-being. He was known – until the 1997-1998 economic crisis – as the 'Father of Development'.

Modern Indonesia

The last decade has seen a transformation in Indonesia's economic and political landscape. No commentator was sufficiently prescient to foresee these changes, and no one knows where, ultimately, they will lead. For the first time since the attempted coup of 1965, Indonesia is entering truly uncharted territory. The chronically pessimistic see Indonesia fragmenting and the economy continuing to bump along the bottom as political instability prevents investor confidence returning. Optimists see stability returning in a brighter post-East Timor/post Suharto era, and economic and investor confidence with it. With Papua clamouring for more autonomy, and resource-rich provinces like Riau and East Kalimantan demanding a larger slice of the pie, the central government in Jakarta is finding it almost impossible to keep people happy.

From 1965 through to 1998, Indonesia was under the control of a military- bureaucratic elite led by President Suharto. Power was exercised through Sekber Golkar, better known as just Golkar, the state's very own political party. In political terms at least, Indonesia was one of the world's most stable countries. It might not have been rich or powerful, but at least there was continuity of leadership. But in 1998 all that changed. Suharto was forced to resign after bitter riots in Jakarta brought on by the collapse of the Indonesian economy, but fuelled by decades of nepotism and corruption. What began as student protests escalated into communal violence and some 1200 people were killed. The critical Chinese community – central to the operation of the economy – fled the country (for the interim at least) and an already dire economic situation became catastrophic. Suharto's vice president, BJ Habibie, took over the helm, but with scarcely a great deal of enthusiasm from the general populace or from the military. Elections were held on 7 June 1999, the first free elections for 44 years, and they were contested by scores of parties. Megawati Sukarnoputri, former president Sukarno's daughter, won the largest share of the vote through her party PDI-Perjuangan (PDI-Struggle). Even with PDI-P's victory, however, some feared that BJ Habibie would call on the political muscle of Golkar to secure him victory in the presidential elections. But the tragedy of East Timor put paid to that and he had to face the humiliation, in October 1999, of a vote of censure and no confidence in the newly muscular and independent People's Consultative Assembly (Indonesia's parliament).

Politics in the post-Suharto era

On 7 June 1999, Indonesians enjoyed their first truly democratic elections since 1955. Despite dire predictions to the contrary, they were largely peaceful. About 112 million votes were cast – 90% of eligible voters – at 250,000 polling stations around the country. A total of 48 parties contested the poll, 45 of them new, and Megawati Sukarnoputri's Democratic Party of Struggle (PDI-P) won the largest share of the vote, attracting 34% of the total. In second place came Golkar with 22%. This was a surprise to some foreign observers, given the bad press Golkar had received, but reflected the party's links with the bureaucracy and a strong showing in the Outer Islands where 'reformasi' had had less of an impact. The three other parties to attract significant numbers of votes were the National Awakening Party (12%), the National Mandate Party (7%) and the United Development Party (10%).

Indonesia's first taste of democracy since 1955 has led to profound changes in the character of both politics and politicians. In the past, MPs had no constituency as such and so were rarely bothered about the need to represent real people. They merely had to make sure they pleased the party bosses. Members of the new parliament, however, not only have responsibilities to their electorates, but are also likely to be much more outspoken.

Because presidents will now have term limits (Suharto was in power for 32 years), this will confer greater power on parliament. As Dan Murphy said in mid-1999 and before the presidential elections, "the next president … will confront populist and legislative challenges like no one has faced since Megawati's father and Indonesia's first president, Sukarno, dispensed with democracy 40 years ago" (FEER, 19.8.99).

Under former President Suharto, **Golkar** was, in effect, the state's own party. All state employees were automatically members of Golkar, and during election campaigns the state controlled the activities of other parties. Not surprisingly, therefore, Golkar was able consistently to win over 60% of the votes cast in parliamentary elections, and controlled the Parliament (DPR) and the People's Consultative Assembly. Even before Suharto's resignation in 1998, there was the enduring sense that the tide of history was running against Golkar. The provinces where Golkar did least well were in the country's heartland – like Jakarta and East Java. It was here, in Java, that Indonesia's middle classes and 'new rich' were beginning to clamour for more of a say in how the country was run, and by whom. With Golkar's loss of the elections of 1999 to the PDI-P, the party has come to accept a new and less central role in the country. In the past all bureaucrats were automatically members of Golkar and were expected to support and represent Golkar. This is no longer the case.

But despite the fact that the PDI-P won the 1999 parliamentary elections, there were commentators who did not think that Megawati, the party's leader, would become president. Prior to the East Timor debacle, some feared that BJ Habibie would ally himself with one or two other parties and use Golkar to gain the presidency against the run of votes. That assumption was shattered when it became clear that the people of East Timor would vote for independence. But Habibie's mistake was not that he failed to control the army and the militias, but that he was foolish enough to offer the East Timorese a referendum on independence in the first place.

In October 1999 the People's Consultative Assembly voted for Indonesia's new president – and it was a cliffhanger. Indonesians could watch – another first for the country – democracy in progress as their representatives lodged their preferences. It was a close contest between Megawati Sukarnoputri, the people's favourite, and the respected **Abdurrahman Wahid**, an almost blind cleric and leader of the country's largest Muslim association, the Nahdlatul Ulama (NU), and a master of the politics of appeasement; a quality which in the President of such a diverse nation can stymie progress and blunt his effectiveness. As it turned out, Wahid won by 373 votes to 313 as he garnered the support of Golkar members and many of those linked to Muslim parties. Initially, Megawati's vociferous and easily agitated supporters rioted when they realized that their leader had been, as they saw it, robbed of her democratic entitlement. Wisely, Wahid asked Megawati to be his vice-president and she asked her supporters to calm down and return home. The election of Wahid and Megawati was, arguably, the best combination that could have been hoped for in the circumstances. It allied a moderate with a populist, and it kept army commander-in-chief General Wiranto out of the two leadership spots (although he was asked to join the cabinet). Wahid's cabinet, announced a few days after the election, showed a desire to calm tensions and promote pragmatic leadership. Significantly, he included two Chinese in his cabinet (one, the critical finance minister), as well as one politician from Aceh and another from West Papua – the two provinces with the greatest secessionist inclinations. On his election to the presidency, four critical questions faced Indonesia's new president. First, how to mend the economy; second, how to keep the country from disintegrating; third, how to promote reconciliation between the different racial and religious groups; and fourth, how to invent a role for the army appropriate for a democratic country entering the 21st century.

Indonesia has changed in other ways – although these changes could be reversed should the move towards democratization begin to falter. For a start, the judiciary and the press are increasingly independent. During the last few years of the Suharto era, hesitant steps towards greater press freedom were often followed by a crackdown on publications deemed to have crossed some ill-defined line in the sand. The independence of the judiciary was, if anything, an even more vexed issue. Political opponents of Suharto and his cronies could not expect a fair trial, and foreign businessmen found using the courts to extract payments from errant Indonesian businessmen and companies a waste of time. In 1997 a clerk at the Supreme Court was heard explaining to a litigant how Indonesia's legal system worked: "If you give us 50 million rupiah but your opponent gives us more, then the case will be won by your opponent" (quoted in *The Economist*, 2000). This approach to legal contests may have the advantage of simplicity, but it hardly instilled a great deal of confidence that a case would be judged on its merits.

In the six months following Suharto's resignation nearly 200 new publications were registered. The government under Habibie was rather more thick-skinned than its predecessor, and in June 1998 a law permitting the Information Ministry to ban any publication for criticizing the government was scrapped. This move towards greater press freedom in the post-Suharto era has meant a much more active, campaigning and, occasionally, sensationalist press – something that President Wahid has sometimes found rather harder to stomach than did Habibie.

Disintegration?

It has long been said that Indonesia is one of the world's most unlikely countries, a patchwork of cultures and languages pieced together by little more than the industriousness of the Dutch. In early 1999 President BJ Habibie, as a sop to the international community, surprisingly offered the people of East Timor a referendum on independence. The UN was called in to supervise the vote on 30 August but, against UN advice and pleading, he refused even a small international peacekeeping force. The vote itself proceeded smoothly and with little intimidation. On 4 September the results of the vote were announced: 78.5% of a turnout of well over 90% chose independence. It seems, and this might seem incredible to anyone who has followed the East Timor story, that the Indonesian military were expecting to 'win' the vote and were piqued that the population were so patently ungrateful for all their hard work. So, with the announcement of the results, mayhem broke out. Militias, formed, encouraged, armed and orchestrated by the Indonesian military, murdered, raped and terrorized the population of the tiny province. Tens of thousands fled to the hills and into neighbouring West Timor. (On 13 September one UN official suggested that just 200,000 out of East Timor's 800,000 population were still living in their homes.) Dili was virtually razed to the ground. The UN compound was besieged. Only the most intense international pressure, and vociferously negative international press coverage, forced Habibie to allow the UN to authorize an Australian-led force to enter the province.

The reluctance of the military to allow East Timor's independence can be linked to two key factors. First, between the annexation of East Timor in 1975 and the referendum of 1999, the army lost perhaps as many as 20,000 men trying to quell the independence movement there. To give up was to admit that it was all a waste of time and blood. And second, and much more importantly, there was the fear that East Timor's independence might herald the break-up of Indonesia. Aceh and Papua were the most obvious provinces that could break away. Legally speaking, there is a clear difference between East Timor and anywhere else in Indonesia. East Timor's annexation by Indonesia was never recognized by the UN. (UN maps always indicated the territory as a separate country.) But the fear was that this nuance would be lost on people with desires for independence.

The 7500-strong Australian-led UN force landed in Dili in late September 1999 and control of the territory passed from the Indonesians to the UN. Alongside the Aussie troops, there were British Gurkhas, New Zealanders, and even contingents from the region, including Thai and Malaysian troops. (Asean came out of the crisis poorly, yet again showing an inability to act in a timely and forceful manner.) Even as UNIFET (the UN International Force for East Timor) strengthened its hold on Dili, the withdrawal of Indonesian troops destroyed the town they had called their own for nearly 25 years. As one soldier told *The Economist*: "We built this place up. Now we've torn it all down again" (02.10.99). During October, UNIFET extended its control east and west from Dili as far as the border with West Timor where the militias were holed up. Rumours of a militia build-up and possible major incursion did not materialize, although there were some firefights between UNIFET and militia gangs. At the end of October Xanana Gusmao, jailed for 20 years by Indonesia and the most likely person to become East Timor's first president, returned home. Before leaving Australia he said: "We will start from zero to reconstruct not only our country, but ourselves as human beings" (*The Economist*, 16.10.99).

A complication – and another reason why the Indonesian army were so reluctant to give up their hold on this dry and poverty-stricken land – was the decision taken by the UN on 27 September 1999 to investigate human rights abuses in the province. And they were right to be worried. When the UN and Indonesian reports were published at the beginning of 2000, six generals were mentioned by name, including General Wiranto (see below).

It was not just East Timor and Aceh that were wracked by violence. Indeed, the spread of unrest to other areas of the country seemed to bear out the army's fears: that taking the lid off more than three decades of top-down control would lead to an upsurge of violence right across the country. Conspiracy theories abounded as to which interested party was seeding this violence. Some believed that much of the unrest was being orchestrated by the military – anxious to prove that without their control the country would disintegrate. Influential individuals from the Suharto era might have been trying to destabilize the country in order to regain power. As criminologist Yohanes Sutoyo explained to Dini Djalal of the *Far Eastern Economic Review*: "The New Order [of former President Suharto] taught us that the only way to solve a problem is with violence", adding, "It is difficult to undo this" (FEER 13.07.2000). At the beginning of 2000, communal violence in the Spice Islands of Maluku escalated and by mid-year an estimated 3000 people had been killed. In Central Sulawesi, murderous groups were killing villagers. In central Kalimantan deadly clashes broke out between indigenous Dayaks and migrants from Madura Island, who came as part of the Suharto government's *transmigrasi* programme. Bali and Lombok were also the scenes of unprecedented violence at the beginning of 2000, some of it aimed at the Chinese community, many of whom are Christians. In Jakarta, and in some other cities on Java, vigilante groups have taken it upon themselves to mete out retribution on small time criminals. Reports of people stealing bicycles being lynched, beaten, doused with kerosene and set alight were common during 2000. The police, in such cases, stood by, powerless to intervene.

While disintegration, partial or otherwise, is a possibility, the government is in the process of introducing laws that will lead to far-reaching **decentralization** to try and head off those who would prefer even greater autonomy. But there are worries that this attempt to devolve power to the provinces will permit local power-brokers to dominate affairs and make corruption even worse. It will also mean that poor provinces such as East and West Nusa Tenggara will no longer be able to rely on cross-subsidization by richer provinces such as Riau and Aceh. Furthermore, it is far from clear that there are sufficient numbers of competent people in the provinces to handle such an increase in the power and role of local level government.

Gus Dur tried to put it back together

President Abdurrahman Wahid, better known as Gus (a term of respect) Dur (from his name), did not have an easy task when he assumed the presidency at the end of 1999.

Gus Dur was renowned for his cunning and wily ways – and his fondness for obtuseness. When he was leader of Nahdlatul Ulama (NU), the world's largest Muslim organization, he was one of President Suharto's very few critics. And he was also able to present himself as a moderate Muslim: one who would protect the interests of Indonesia's non-Muslim population while remaining a respected Muslim cleric, leader and thinker. In January 2000 he travelled to Saudi Arabia to court the Arab world and then flew to Davos in Switzerland for the World Economic Forum. Here he met with Prime Minister Barak of Israel and George Soros. He explained: "We need investments and, you know, the Jewish community everywhere are very active in the commercial side ..." (FEER 10.02.2000). His critics said he undermined Indonesia's stability and economic recovery by his impulsiveness; he frequently made statements without consulting his cabinet (as happened when he said, while on an overseas trip, that General Wiranto should resign) and people also complained of his readiness to blame conspirators for the country's problems. His supporters believed he was a great master who disarmed his opponents by his seeming foolishness, before bringing them down. With few political cards to play, once many in his coalition government turned against him, his defenders believed that speaking out was his only weapon. Without the backing of a fully functioning bureaucracy, or the military power used by his predecessor, his force of personality and ability to bluff were the only tools at his disposal.

His greatest victory, or so it seemed at the time, was to sideline the army and emasculate its leadership as a political force. This also showed him at his wily best. Initially, Wahid included General Wiranto, the army's powerful chief of staff, in his cabinet, but not, significantly, as defence minister. Instead he appointed him as security minister. This helped to separate the General from his power base. Then the president said that he would sack anyone implicated in human rights abuses in East Timor. Reports commissioned by the Indonesian government and by the UN into just this issue were released on 31 January 2000. Moreover, both came to the same conclusion: that members of the Indonesian army had assisted the militias in East Timor to murder, rape and pillage. More to the point, the Indonesian report mentioned six generals by name, including General Wiranto. The president was abroad at the time but in an interview said he thought that Wiranto should resign. Instead the General pointedly turned up at a cabinet meeting. However, having initially said that the General could stay, he changed his mind once more and sacked the general from his post as security minister (although he remained an 'inactive' member of the cabinet). Cut off from the army and in a government post with no significance, General Wiranto was successfully trapped in a no man's land of Gus Dur's making.

But Wahid did not just get rid of Wiranto. He appointed a civilian as minister of defence and promoted officers in the navy and airforce to influential positions, thus downgrading the traditionally highly dominant army. This culminated in a major reshuffle at the end of

February 2000. Furthermore, Wahid insisted that military men in the cabinet had to resign from their military posts before taking up their political appointments.

While Gus Dur sidelined the army, he didn't counted on the public taking up arms to deal with the problems of the nation (probably orcestrated from above – possibly by factions of the army). At the beginning of 2000, as Muslim-Christian violence in Maluku escalated, radical Muslims in Java began to prepare for a *jihad* (holy war) in this far-flung province. White-robed warriors in their thousands, some wielding swords, congregated in Jakarta to make their feelings clear – and then began to train for battle. Despite Gus Dur's attempts to stop them leaving for Maluku, they began to arrive in the region by the end of May 2000. As the year wore on it became increasingly clear that Wahid's victory over the generals was a pyrrhic one. Infuriated by the president's actions, the army began to undermine his leadership. In particular, a series of bombings in Jakarta would seem to involve the army, or groups in the army. By the end of 2000 the army seemed to be clawing back power.

During the course of 2000, many people who initially welcomed Wahid's accession to the presidency became increasingly disenchanted with his leadership – and with his methods. In an attempt to address this mounting criticism, he proposed far-reaching changes to the management of state affairs. In effect he proposed a more equal, four-way sharing of power between his marginalized Vice President Megawati Sukarnoputri, two new 'Coordinating' ministers, and himself. The two coordinating ministers were later announced as being Sulsilo Bambang Yudhoyono, a retired general, and Rizal Ramli. Significantly, neither of these two men had prior links with any political party. Under this system Wahid would become, in effect, Indonesia's face to the wider world: a sort of roving ambassador for the country. Wahid claimed in the speech that he was ceding 'duties and not authority', but the distinction was a fine one.

Wahid's proposed changes were tacit acceptance on his part that he had lost his way. It sometimes seemed, in the months leading up to the August 2000 meeting, that Wahid lacked the clarity of mind to address key issues, and especially those of an economic flavour. His woolly pronouncements and tendency to prevaricate exasperated many businessmen and foreign investors.

Towards the end of 2000, Indonesia continued to lurch from crisis to crisis, both economically and politically. President Abdurrahman Wahid became increasingly embattled as his problems mounted. In particular, he seemed to have lost control of the army and the police who were, apparently, ignoring or going against his orders. This extended from his order for the army and police to crack down on the militias in West Timor (following the murder of three UN personnel there); to his demand that Tommy Suharto, one of former President Suharto's sons, be arrested in connection with a spate of bombings in Jakarta (the police released him saying there was not sufficient evidence); to a ceasefire in the northern Sumatran province of Aceh, which the army also apparently chose to ignore. Some commentators wondered whether the army was once more out of control and it was even suggested that Wahid could be toppled by an army-inspired coup.

Domestic hangovers and international relations

Indonesia's acceptance into the international fold has been hampered for years by numerous small and large stumbling blocks. The 'occupation' of East Timor, government policy in Papua, corruption, the nature of the political system, the failure to respect labour rights, and the human and environmental impacts of the transmigration programme, terrorist attaccks on Western targets, to name just a few. Just when Indonesia is on the verge of expunging the stain on its credibility, one or more of these issues jumps out and progress is stymied.

There can be no doubt that the major stumbling block was East Timor. Even before the tragic events which followed the vote for independence in mid-1999, East Timor was a thorn in Indonesia's attempts to punch its weight. (For a country of over 200,000,000 people, the fourth most populous on earth, it has a remarkably low international profile.) Nationalist sentiment was stoked by the presence of UN forces in East Timor (widely seen to be Australian forces in East Timor), and Indonesia's failure to come to terms with its misguided imperialist spree raised the stakes still further. At the end of September 1999, US Secretary of Defence William Cohen warned that Indonesia could face 'political isolation' and 'economic consequences' if it did not control its military.

Large chinks began forming in the armour of Wahid's popular support. In 2001, as he pushed for further reconciliation with separatists in Papua and Aceh, martial law was imposed in Maluku as fighting between Christians and Muslims intensified. It was discovered that the government ordered the military to block all members of Laskar Jihad (an Islamist group made up of Muslims from across the archipelago) from travelling to Maluku to fight. Not only did the military fail to do this, it soon became clear that Laskar Jihad was being funded by the Indonesian military. Things got worse for Wahid when he became embroiled in two huge financial scandals involving large sums of money that went missing from the State Logistics Agency (the money – US$4 million – was found with Wahid's masseur) and from a donation given by the Sultan of Brunei.

After legalising the use of Chinese characters and making Chinese New Year a national holiday in January 2001, Wahid declared at a meeting of university rectors that if Indonesia fell into a state of anarchy, he would be forced to consider dissolving the DPR (House of Representatives), a remark that won him few friends. At a special convening of the DPR a memorandum was signed against Wahid. A second would force a Special Session in which the impeachment and removal of a president would be a legal action. The writing was on the wall for the President and in April as his NU (Nahdlatul Ulama – Wahid's Islamic group) offered to fight to the end in support of their president, it seemed as though the nation was again slipping into grave civil strife. A second memorandum against Wahid was written after he sacked two members of his own cabinet as dissidents. Wahid was growing desperate and demanded that Susilo Bambang Yudhyono (then Minister for Security) call a state of emergency, a request which was refused. The date of MPR (People's Consultative Assembly) session for the impeachment of Wahid was hurried forward and the Indonesian army rallied against the president, flooding Jakarta with troops and aiming their tanks at the presidential palace. The MPR declared the end of Wahid's term as president, which he initially refused to accept, before finally conceding and slipping off to the USA for medical reasons.

In July 2001 Megawati Soekarno-Putri took over the reigns of power. She was seen to take a very passive role, enjoying her status as a daughter of the cult figure and founding father of Indonesia, Soekarno. It was noted by critics that she seemed more interested in developing her hobbies of gardening and watching cartoons than intervening in government business. Three years after she had taken power, elections were called and although the economic situation had improved slightly, rates of poverty and unemployment remained high. It was during her reign that terrorists struck foreign targets Bali and Jakarta, prompting falling confidence from foreign investors and once again thrusting Indonesia into the international headlines for all the wrong reasons. Megawati lost the election to Susilo Bambang Yudhyono (SBY), and quietly left the palace.

Yudhyono was thrust into the deep end after he had won the election Indonesia was devastated by the Boxing Day tsunami off Aceh. This blow was followed by the earthquake in Bantul, several more along the coast of West Sumatra, the eruption of

Gunung Merapi and another deadly tsunami off Pangandaran. This series of natural disasters put an immense strain on the country and its leadership. This was only exaggerated by the 2005 suicide attacks in Bali. Yudhyono promised to track down the perpetrators with his forces managing to track down and kill Dr Azahari, one of the ringleaders of the attack, in Malang. The police scored another success in September 2009 when they managed to kill another key player, Noordin M Top, on a raid in a house just outside Solo. Azahari and Top were thought to be the masterminds behind the Bali bombings, the JW Marriot bombings and the Australian embassy bombings in Jakarta. After years of legal wrangling, the three Bali bombers, Imam Samudra, Mukhlas and Amrozi were executed by firing squad in November 2008 in Central Java. Their bodies were flown by helicopter to their homes in Java where they received emotional burials suggesting that there are at least a few who agree with their deeds.

In July 2009 Indonesia held its presidential election to cover the country's leadership from 2009 to 2014. This was the second election where citizens voted directly for the president and vice-president and was won convincingly by Yudhyono and his vice president Boediono with over 60% of the vote.

Contents

Footnotes

Index

Titles available in the Footprint *Focus* range

Latin America	UK RRP	US RRP
Bahia & Salvador	£7.99	$11.95
Brazilian Amazon	£7.99	$11.95
Brazilian Pantanal	£6.99	$9.95
Buenos Aires & Pampas	£7.99	$11.95
Cartagena & Caribbean Coast	£7.99	$11.95
Costa Rica	£8.99	$12.95
Cuzco, La Paz & Lake Titicaca	£8.99	$12.95
El Salvador	£5.99	$8.95
Guadalajara & Pacific Coast	£6.99	$9.95
Guatemala	£8.99	$12.95
Guyana, Guyane & Suriname	£5.99	$8.95
Havana	£6.99	$9.95
Honduras	£7.99	$11.95
Nicaragua	£7.99	$11.95
Northeast Argentina & Uruguay	£8.99	$12.95
Paraguay	£5.99	$8.95
Quito & Galápagos Islands	£7.99	$11.95
Recife & Northeast Brazil	£7.99	$11.95
Rio de Janeiro	£8.99	$12.95
São Paulo	£5.99	$8.95
Uruguay	£6.99	$9.95
Venezuela	£8.99	$12.95
Yucatán Peninsula	£6.99	$9.95

Asia	UK RRP	US RRP
Angkor Wat	£5.99	$8.95
Bali & Lombok	£8.99	$12.95
Chennai & Tamil Nadu	£8.99	$12.95
Chiang Mai & Northern Thailand	£7.99	$11.95
Goa	£6.99	$9.95
Gulf of Thailand	£8.99	$12.95
Hanoi & Northern Vietnam	£8.99	$12.95
Ho Chi Minh City & Mekong Delta	£7.99	$11.95
Java	£7.99	$11.95
Kerala	£7.99	$11.95
Kolkata & West Bengal	£5.99	$8.95
Mumbai & Gujarat	£8.99	$12.95

Africa & Middle East	UK RRP	US RRP
Beirut	£6.99	$9.95
Cairo & Nile Delta	£8.99	$12.95
Damascus	£5.99	$8.95
Durban & KwaZulu Natal	£8.99	$12.95
Fès & Northern Morocco	£8.99	$12.95
Jerusalem	£8.99	$12.95
Johannesburg & Kruger National Park	£7.99	$11.95
Kenya's Beaches	£8.99	$12.95
Kilimanjaro & Northern Tanzania	£8.99	$12.95
Luxor to Aswan	£8.99	$12.95
Nairobi & Rift Valley	£7.99	$11.95
Red Sea & Sinai	£7.99	$11.95
Zanzibar & Pemba	£7.99	$11.95

Europe	UK RRP	US RR
Bilbao & Basque Region	£6.99	$9.95
Brittany West Coast	£7.99	$11.95
Cádiz & Costa de la Luz	£6.99	$9.95
Granada & Sierra Nevada	£6.99	$9.95
Languedoc: Carcassonne to Montpellier	£7.99	$11.95
Málaga	£5.99	$8.95
Marseille & Western Provence	£7.99	$11.95
Orkney & Shetland Islands	£5.99	$8.95
Santander & Picos de Europa	£7.99	$11.95
Sardinia: Alghero & the North	£7.99	$11.95
Sardinia: Cagliari & the South	£7.99	$11.95
Seville	£5.99	$8.95
Sicily: Palermo & the Northwest	£7.99	$11.95
Sicily: Catania & the Southeast	£7.99	$11.95
Siena & Southern Tuscany	£7.99	$11.95
Sorrento, Capri & Amalfi Coast	£6.99	$9.95
Skye & Outer Hebrides	£6.99	$9.95
Verona & Lake Garda	£7.99	$11.95

North America	UK RRP	US RRP
Vancouver & Rockies	£8.99	$12.95

Australasia	UK RRP	US RRP
Brisbane & Queensland	£8.99	$12.95
Perth	£7.99	$11.95

For the latest books, e-books and a wealth of travel information, visit us at: www.footprinttravelguides.com.

 footprinttravelguides.com

Join us on facebook for the latest travel news, product releases, offers and amazing competitions: www.facebook.com/footprintbooks.